Rediscoving
Black Conservatism

By Lee H. Walker

Rediscovering
Black Conservatism

Published by The Heartland Institute
19 South LaSalle Street #903
Chicago, Illinois 60603
phone 312/377-4000
fax 312/377-5000
www.heartland.org

Additional copies of this book
are available from The Heartland Institute
for the following prices:

1-10 copies	$8.95 per copy
11-50 copies	$7.95 per copy
51-100 copies	$6.95 per copy
101 or more	$5.95 per copy

Printed in the United States of America
ISBN-13 978-1-934791-27-1
ISBN-10 1-934791-27-x

Manufactured in the United States of America

Contents

Inspiration

We are so anxious to solve the race problem that we do not take time to study it. - *Kelly Miller*

To an academician, history is the pursuit of truth, no matter where the truth leads, because we believe the truth is a liberating factor in itself. - *Benjamin Quarles*

I learned how to size up a situation and determine if it advanced my interests. This was perhaps the most important lesson of all, for our destiny is, in large part, in our own hands. - *John H. Johnson*

No greater injury can be done to any youth, than to let him feel that because he belongs to this or that race he will be advanced in life regardless of his own merits or efforts. - *Booker T. Washington*

Those who think there is no opportunity for them to live grandly, yea, heroically, no matter how lowly their calling, no matter how humble their surroundings, make a common but very serious error. - *Booker T. Washington*

To those of my race who depend on bettering their condition in a foreign land, or who underestimate the importance of preserving friendly relations with the southern white man who is their next door neighbor, I would say: "Cast down your bucket where you are." Cast it down, making friends in every manly way of the people of all races, by whom you are surrounded. - *Booker T. Washington*

Introduction

This book offers a balanced historical perspective on black Americans' social, religious, and political thought after the Civil War until 1915, and then up to the present. It is intended to serve as an antidote to a lopsided view of black America that historians have promulgated during the twentieth century.

Black Americans' views on politics and culture have been more diverse over the years than many people may realize. These views developed from a strongly middle-class and openly spiritual culture in the 1880s, which became the foundation of a black middle-class that could survive in a world of significantly altered racial relationships after the collapse of Reconstruction.

Radicals or Conservatives?

There have been two main views of blacks' political and social position in the United States and how to improve the lot of black Americans. These were described effectively by Kelly Miller, dean and professor of sociology at Howard University and one of the foremost black intellectuals in the early years of the twentieth century.

Miller noted that the leading black voices in 1900 were Booker T. Washington and W. E. B. DuBois. He described Washington and his followers as conservatives, and DuBois and his followers as radicals. In 1908, Miller published his findings in a book titled *Radicals & Conservatives*.[1] He noted that both groups agreed on the end in view for blacks, but differed over the most effective means of attaining it.

Recognizing the seeming incongruity between conservatism as it was

---

[1] Kelly Miller, *Radicals & Conservatives and Other Essays on the Negro in America* (New York: Schocken Books, 1968).

generally defined and the desperate plight of black people, Miller told this amusing story:

> When a distinguished Russian was informed that some American Negroes are radical and some conservative, he could not restrain his laughter. The idea of conservative Negroes was more than the Cossack's risibilities could endure. "What on earth," he exclaimed with astonishment, "have they to conserve?"[2]

But blacks, even in the early part of the twentieth century, had much to conserve. They sought to conserve their faith, families, culture, and their newly won freedom.

While the radicals more visibly called for changes in the social order, conservative blacks were by no means accommodationists. Throughout this nation's history, some of the greatest agents of change in black America have been conservative. Nevertheless, the public presentation of the debate between "conservatism" and "radicalism" among blacks has all too often been one-sided, generally omitting the conservative side.

For example, President Bill Clinton approved a national study of black Americans headed by the noted and well-respected John Hope Franklin, Ph.D., a former professor of history at the University of Chicago. Franklin refused to include conservative blacks in his study. After much debate, he interviewed only a few such individuals. Jay Parker of the Lincoln Institute in Washington, D.C., writes that the refusal to include conservatives in the discussion of black aims and strategies "reveals an almost total lack of understanding and awareness of blacks in American history and of black intellectual tradition in the United States."

What Does it Mean to Be a Conservative Black?

As a result of this suppression of differing points of view, conservative attitudes among black Americans have been publicized during only a few historical periods in the United States in the years since the Civil War. Most of the time, the major emphasis has been on forcing racial integration and assimilation through political means.

This contrast between politics and the conservative emphasis on

---

[2] Ibid., p. 25.

economics and culture, clearly identified by Miller, is why I use the term conservative as an adjective, not a noun, when describing black American attitudes. The term is intended to describe a worldview and a culture, not a defined, partisan political position. It represents more of an attitude than a political affiliation.

I was born and reared in the Deep South, in the state of Alabama during the era of legal segregation under Jim Crow. Despite the poor treatment we received at the hands of much of society and especially the government, which forced segregation throughout society, Southern blacks viewed life through a fundamentally conservative lens, and our leadership's ultimate goal was to abolish legal segregation and second-class citizenship. Thus my conservatism is in the tradition of Booker T. Washington and Frederick Douglass.

Conservative attitudes like my own are quite common among black Americans. Most conservative blacks are middle-class, with a strong religious foundation, but this attitude exists in all classes. During the past century, the greatest number of conservative black Americans was in the South, because that is where 90 percent of the blacks lived through slavery and the first decades of the twentieth century. Kelley Miller noted this reality in *Radicals & Conservatives*, and the South remains a bastion of black conservatism today.

After a great migration north during the middle of the twentieth century (which concentrated blacks in some of the Northern urban strongholds of political liberalism), however, the twenty-first century trend in black migration is back to the South, in response to the high crime and drug abuse rates and poor education systems in most Northern cities. While most whites and many blacks are aware of the Congressional Back Caucus in Washington, they may not know that the Southern blacks tend to identify themselves with the Blue Dog Democrats, the conservatives. House Speaker Nancy Pelosi describes them as "important voices in our diverse caucus." All of this suggests that conservative attitudes may well become even stronger among black Americans in years to come.

Rediscovery and a New Debate

The current rediscovery and debate over black Americans' history and culture began in 1980 with the Black Alternatives Conference in San Francisco. The gathering was convened by Dr. Henry Lucas and Thomas

Sowell, Ph.D., an economist at the Hoover Institution at Stanford University. It was the first time in history since Booker T. Washington's death in 1915 that a group of predominantly black Americans had met to discuss the impact of liberal policies on the black community.

I was part of that group of about three hundred people from across the country, which included Democrats, Republicans, and independents, and both blacks and whites. The conference led to the founding of an organization, The New Coalition for Economic and Social Change, headed first by Clarence Pendleton, Jr. I later took over its leadership and moved the organization's headquarters from California to Chicago, Illinois.

Charles V. Hamilton, former political science professor at Columbia University, wrote in 1982, "throughout 1981, there was substantial attention paid to those blacks who generally supported the policies of the conservative [Reagan] administration. This is an understandable interest, given the history of mass black opinion and political behavior which is noted for its liberal, not conservative, preferences."[3]

Other scholars are coming to see black conservatism as a serious force. Princeton American history professor Nell Irvin Painter devotes several pages to black conservatism in her latest book, *Creating Black Americans,* under the heading "Black Conservatives Gain Prominence." Rhett S. Jones, professor of history at Brown University, has done research on the eighteenth century origins of black American conservatism, which was published in my organization's newsletter.

Plan of the Book

I attempt in this book to define and discuss the conservative viewpoints that a considerable number of blacks have thought and expressed since the late 1880s. It is not a systematic treatise but rather a primer on black conservatism, examining the intersection of conservatism and the black community from a variety of different angles.

The first two chapters are primarily historical, briefly tracing the black conservative impulse through our nation's beginnings, and looking specifically at the role of Booker T. Washington. The next three chapters

---

[3] Annual Report on State of Black America, National Urban League, 1982.

address the three core components of Dr. Washington's philosophy: education, entrepreneurship, and self-reliance. The final three chapters examine the failure of America's black leadership, profile prominent black conservative individuals on the scene today, and outline a conservative perspective on contemporary issues.

The United States has changed greatly since the years of my childhood, exemplified by the election of a black man to the highest office in the land just a month before this book went to press. Whatever else it may say, it is clear that the election of Barack Obama signifies the full inclusion of black Americans into the nation's political process and a new day for relations among people of different colors in the United States.

A hundred years ago President Theodore Roosevelt invited Booker T. Washington to dinner at the White House and caused a racial storm throughout the South. Now we have a black president, who garnered millions of votes from the white South, welcoming guests at the White House.

While the election of President Obama completes the political integration of blacks into American society and is greatly to be applauded for that, the hard work of integrating black Americans into the nation's economy and social structures remains to be done. By avoiding the twin traps of isolation from whites and dependence on whites, blacks can complete the final leg of the journey to equality and prosperity.

Chapter 1

Black Conservatism - History and Future

Over the past thirty years, billions of dollars have been poured into black communities across the country in hope of curing a host of well-documented socioeconomic problems, including failing schools, inadequate housing, rampant crime and drug abuse, black-on-black killings, unemployment and more. Despite the courageous efforts of many local institutions, agencies, school leaders, grassroots organizations, and community residents, the problems remain. In many instances, they have grown worse. I believe it will take new ideas and new voices to find solutions.

For more than fifty years, black Americans have been viewed as being political liberals. Politicians who espouse liberal ideas have generally captured both the imagination and the votes of blacks. The belief that all blacks are liberals is further supported by the statements and actions of most prominent black leaders and spokespersons. Their positions on policy issues are generally considered by the media as representing the attitudes and opinions of all blacks in the country. However, polls show that the majority of blacks do not hold the same views as these leaders. For example, a 1992 survey showed that 32 percent of U.S. blacks characterized themselves as conservative, 31 percent as moderate, and only 36 percent as liberal.[4]

An example getting a lot of attention recently is "school choice," such as the plan to give vouchers to families so that the children can attend schools of the parents' choice. Nearly 60 percent of black parents want vouchers, as they provide an opportunity to get their children a good education in places with failing public schools.[5] Liberal black leaders,

---

[4] *National Public Opinion Survey 1992*, The Joint Center for Political and Economic Studies, 1992.

[5] *2000 National Opinion Poll - Politics*, The Joint Center for Political and Economic Studies, 2000

however, strongly oppose school choice because of their connections with teachers unions.

The same dynamic holds true for many other issues, in which the black population largely just wants an opportunity to work hard and enjoy the rewards of their efforts, while black leaders work to use government to extract subsidies, grants and favors - continually characterized as payment for past injustices-from the rest of society. There is, however, nothing particularly African-American about this passion for government solutions. Black conservatism has been an overlooked aspect of American history since the collapse of Reconstruction. Any comprehensive history of black American thought that ignores or isolates the conservative influence will be incomplete and unbalanced.

For the past sixty-five years, the liberals who ran the most visible black organizations omitted the ideas and contributions of black conservatives. Their focus was on integration. There is nothing wrong with integration, but it should have been the result, rather than the goal of social action. The previous black movement, led by Booker T. Washington, had been about self-sufficiency and business development.

The values and principles of black conservatism are rooted in what Thomas Jefferson and Abraham Lincoln advocated and represented-the rights of liberty and equality before the law, as set forth in the Declaration of Independence. White conservatives writing about American conservatism also have ignored the black influence on the conservative movement during this time. Blacks, however, were just as involved in the conservative movement as they were in the religious movements of the time.

The emergence of black conservatives in the twenty-seven years since Ronald Reagan's election in 1980 has surprised liberal black leaders as well as the media. From a historical point of view, however, black conservatism is not such an unusual phenomenon as most critics, including many academics, claim. It has deep roots within the black community.

Closet Conservatives

Although many liberal scholars proclaimed conservatism dead in the 1940s and 1950s, the resurgence of conservatism is now a recognized fact. Without a doubt, the United States has become more conservative over the past thirty years. Elections since 1980 and opinion polls both support his assertion.[6]

Even in Chicago, a city well-known for its liberal inclinations, blacks have repeatedly identified themselves as conservative. From 1990 through 1994, Northwestern University conducted a survey, the Chicago Area Survey Project, in which researchers asked citizens about their political orientation and affiliation. In 1994, fully 72 percent of blacks surveyed identified themselves as Democrats, and only 4 percent identified themselves as Republicans.[7] In terms of political orientation, however, 46 percent of blacks self-identified as either slightly conservative, conservative, or extremely conservative, and another 10 percent called themselves middle of the road/moderate. Although the Republican label clearly did not sit well with blacks throughout the 1980s, '90s, and early part of this decade, blacks have been very comfortable with conservatism.

Black Americans, including academics, can no longer afford to boycott the larger conservative movement. As has been noted frequently, blacks' passionate loyalty to the Democratic Party allows that party to ignore their concerns, as when Democrats work intensively to block school choice. All other ethnic groups are allowing themselves to be courted; only blacks have closed and, in some cases, locked the door to political competition. This is not just a case of losing an opportunity; it is self-sabotage directed by America's black leadership. What's at stake here is much larger than what political party the majority of blacks belong to. It's about whether blacks can have any real influence in the political process at all.

What Does "Black Conservatism" Mean?

Research shows that conservatism in the black community relates more to traditional middle-class values and morality than to political affiliation. Most white conservatives are Republicans, or vote Republican most frequently, while very few conservative blacks vote Republican. One could

---

[6] Since 1980, conservative candidates have won five out of seven presidential campaigns, and the conservative leaning Republican Party acquired a majority in Congress in 1994 - the first time in over 60 years - and maintained that majority until 2006.

[7] *Chicago Area Survey Project*, Northwestern University Survey Laboratory, 1994

almost say conservative blacks are politically homeless.

Black conservatism is best understood as a state of mind and a type of character, a way of looking at the social order. It is not membership in a club or political party. Nor is it an ideology. It is, instead, a set of traditional principles and a philosophy centered on freedom and virtue. I believe the word "conservative" is best used as an adjective and not a noun. Conservative Americans want to preserve the best of the past and make improvements; conservatism does not contemplate radical change unless the times demand it.

In 1908, Kelly Miller, the first black scholar to graduate from Johns Hopkins University, and who later became dean of Howard University, wrote an essay titled "Radicals and Conservatives." Miller described the followers of Booker T. Washington as conservatives, perhaps the first time anyone had identified the existence of an authentically black conservatism. Booker T. described conservatism as follows: "The Negro should acquire property, own his own land, drive his own mule hitched to his own wagon, milk his own cow, raise his own crop and keep out of debt, and when he acquired a home he became fit for a conservative citizen."

George S. Schuyler, a columnist for the *Pittsburgh Courier*, also described the American black as a conservative, in his 1966 autobiography, *Black and Conservative*: "The American Negro is a prime example of the survival of the fittest.... He has been the outstanding example of American conservatism: adjustable, resourceful, adaptable, patient, and restrained."

Discussing the similarities and differences between white and black conservatism is similar to discussing how black and white Christians differ. They may belong to the same denomination and even the same church, but when they attend church on Sunday mornings, the service and the experiences may be very different. Yet the doctrines and the principles are the same.

A conservative black's overriding interest is in preserving and extending liberty and freedom as expressed in the Declaration of Independence. Being familiar with the long history in which freedom was denied to our ancestors, parents, and even to us in our own lives, we are especially sensitive to threats to it today. You might say that history has made blacks experts on reclaiming freedoms. We do not need to read white economists or political philosophers to teach us about what it is like to be deprived of basic freedoms. Our first concern when addressing public policy is always, "Are we maximizing individual liberty?" Conservative blacks believe liberty is a prerequisite for justice. We never want to debase the dignity of any human being.

These are fundamental conservative principles. As Russell Kirk wrote of the eighteenth-century English philosopher and legislator Edmund Burke in *The Conservative Mind*, "All his life, Burke's chief concern had been for justice and liberty, which must stand or fall together-liberty under law, a definite liberty, the limits of which were determined by prescription. He had defended the liberties of Englishmen against their king, and the liberties of Americans against king and parliament, and the liberties of Hindus against Europeans. He had defended those liberties not because they were innovations, discovered in the Age of Reason, but because they were ancient prerogatives, guaranteed by immemorial usage."[8]

As Burke recognized, liberty has strong foundations in the people's religious faith and social institutions, what he called the "little platoons" of society.[9] American blacks exemplify this reality. The oldest and still most important conservative institution in black America is the church. That is where much of our leadership came from, where many of the first schools open to blacks were housed, and where many fine schools serve black students across the country today. In many black communities, churches serve as engines of economic development, too. Both the black church and private church schools are conservative institutions within the black community.

Black Americans utilized the conservative philosophy that developed there to build churches, insurance companies, and colleges in the South and to develop practical skills during the era of Jim Crow. American history verifies the progress of black America before the 1930s through conservative values. For example, in the post Civil-War South, black incomes rose faster than white incomes for several straight decades, as blacks created businesses, joined the professions, held political office, helped win World War I, and played a key role in the redevelopment of the South. Conservative blacks figured prominently in all of these achievements.

---

[8] Russell Kirk, *The Conservative Mind* (Chicago, IL: Henry Regnery Company, 1953)

[9] Edmund Burke, *Reflections on the Revolution in France*, 1790.

Conservatism in Black History

While black conservatism is by no means a new mindset, much of the past fifty years it has been dismissed as an oxymoron or something less than a respectable point of view. Jay Parker, founder of the Lincoln Institute in Washington, D.C., says, "The very idea of black conservatism seems unreal to some observers, both black and white. This reveals an almost total lack of awareness and understanding of black history and the black intellectual tradition in the United States."

According to historian Peter Eisenstadt, "The recent emergence of conservative blacks provides an opportunity to take a long overdue look at the history of conservative thought among black Americans. Its history is long, and its impact has been persuasive. Any comprehensive history of black American thought that ignores the conservative impulse will be one-sided."[10] Explicitly conservative writing by black thinkers and leaders dates back at least to the 1880s. Conservative and middle-class blacks have generally had a healthy appreciation for and belief in market capitalism and skepticism toward relying on government instead of themselves.

Black Americans have participated in and been affected in one way or another by all social and economic movements in America. The first person to die for American independence, for example, was a black man named Crispus Attucks. In 1770 he was part of a crowd in Boston that was fired upon by British Redcoats in what historians now call the "Boston Massacre." The incident helped ignite the movement for independence. He remained a symbol of liberty for many years after the Revolutionary War.

Bishop Richard Allen, a former slave and founder of the African Methodist Episcopal Church in 1816, was a successful businessman and conservative thinker. His entrepreneurial efforts and strict moral code formed the basis of the moral discourse for much of the black church. Examples like these demonstrate that freedom and economic opportunity for blacks have deep roots in American history. Slavery and servitude are not the only historically significant realities for black America.

One of black conservatism's leading lights was Alexander Crummell, born in New York City in 1819, a Harvard graduate, ordained an Episcopal priest, and founder of a church in Washington, D.C. He also founded the

---

[10] Peter Eisenstadt, "Southern Black Conservatism, 1865-1945: An Introduction," in *Black Conservatism: Essays in Intellectual and Political History*, ed. by Peter Eisenstadt, 1999.

American Negro Academy in 1897, a forum for black intellectuals. Crummell wanted blacks to participate fully in the riches of Western Civilization in a distinctly black way. He worked for years to recruit free blacks to Liberia, where he hoped to create a black colony founded upon Christian principles. When the Liberian experiment failed, Crummell returned to the United States and focused his efforts on expanding educational opportunities for blacks.

Crummell was the first black American to construct an openly conservative political program. In describing the essence of black conservatism, he observed that some black Americans "should be ranked among conservative men in this country, and stand among the firmest upholders of law and authority. They should be counted as the constant foe of revolution, communism, and revolt."[11] Crummell's hero was Alexander Hamilton, and he criticized Thomas Jefferson and the Declaration of Independence for asserting that government derives its consent from the governed rather than from God.

The other prominent black leader of the mid 19th century was the fiery abolitionist Frederick Douglass (1818-1895). Douglass minced no words when denouncing the atrocity of American slavery, and believed that by allowing it to persist America was committing crimes more evil than those of any other nation on earth. In perhaps his most famous speech, "What to the Slave is the 4th of July?" Douglass roared:

> Whether we turn to the declarations of the past, or to the professions of the present, the conduct of the nation seems equally hideous and revolting. America is false to the past, false to the present, and solemnly binds herself to be false to the future. Standing with God and the crushed and bleeding slave on this occasion, I will, in the name of humanity which is outraged, in the name of liberty which is fettered, in the name of the constitution and the Bible, which are disregarded and trampled upon, dare to call in question and to denounce, with all the emphasis I can command, everything that served to perpetuate slavery - the great sin and shame of America!"[12]

---

[11] Ibid.

[12] Frederick Douglass, "What to the Slave is the 4th of July?" (Presented to the United States Congress, Washington, DC, July 5, 1852).

Despite his invective against American slavery, however, Douglass continued to believe in the principles enshrined in the Declaration of Independence. His dream was not to incite a slave revolt or to turn blacks against whites in a perpetual race war. Rather, he urged America to live up to its creed - the belief that all men are created equal - and extend to blacks the rights white Americans had won for themselves. By tying black aspirations for freedom to quintessentially American ideals, Douglass demonstrated his conservatism. His fight was not with Western Civilization or "European Values" but with the hypocrisy of slavery in a country founded upon liberty and equality.

One of Douglass' most significant intellectual transitions involved his views on the United States Constitution. Douglass had originally followed William Lloyd Garrison in holding that the Constitution was a pro-slavery document. After the publication of Lysander Spooner's book *The Unconstitutionality of Slavery*, however, Douglass became persuaded that the Constitution was an inherently anti-slavery document. For the rest of his public life Douglass championed a constitutional approach to emancipation, enfranchisement and civil rights. In contrast to contemporary black liberals, Douglass did not believe Western Civilization was inherently flawed or that America was irredeemably evil. He believed the slavery and racism were extreme defects in an otherwise admirable society and form of government.

Douglass also became a proponent of black self-help during the tumultuous days of reconstruction and the rise of Jim Crow laws in the South. He urged emancipated blacks to seize the opportunities before them without looking to whites for salvation. Douglass certainly remained an advocate of full political equality his entire life, but he placed his hope for black advancement in the individual initiative of blacks, not in the government.

Black Conservatism After Slavery

One of the perpetual disagreements that arose within the ranks of black conservatives took place first between Alexander Crummell and Booker T. Washington (1856-1915). Crummell criticized Washington for not making political and legal equality a priority equal to education and economic progress. It was a major disagreement between Northern and Southern conservative blacks, but for many years Washington's position was more popular. As Kelly Miller wrote in 1908, "Washington had, by far, the largest group of followers, which included the business class, educators and the masses."

After slavery ended, many slaves were surprisingly well-prepared to become free and independent people. Many knew how to read and write, even though it had been against the law for whites to teach them these skills. In addition, many slaves had specialized skills and knowledge that allowed them to start their own businesses and otherwise earn a living without being dependent on their former owners.

Born a slave in the South, Booker T. Washington rose to become one of the greatest thinkers and social reformers of the nineteenth and twentieth centuries. He was - and remains - a personal hero for millions of black Americans. He is a southern black Horatio Alger, the humble and poor black boy who became world-famous as an educator, entrepreneur, and black leader. Washington was the voice of blacks in America for over 20 years and he recruited and trained a cadre of other conservative black thinkers and leaders to help his people rise up from slavery.

One of Washington's proteges was Robinson Taylor (1868-1942), the first black to attend the prestigious Massachusetts Institute of Technology. He enrolled in 1888 and quickly distinguished himself as a gifted and hardworking architect. Booker T. Washington recruited Taylor to Tuskegee after he graduated from MIT, and Taylor became the school architect and director of mechanical studies.

It was during his time at Tuskegee that Taylor fully blossomed as both an architect and a teacher. He designed and constructed the impressive brick buildings that transformed Tuskegee into a world class university. Taylor's architectural prowess contributed to the selection of Tuskegee as a National Historic Site. He instilled in the students his passion for architecture and his uncompromising love of perfection. Taylor also espoused the creed of self-reliance preached by Booker T. Washington. Not only did the students use their newly acquired skills to design and build the structures, they made nearly all of the bricks as well.

In reflecting on his own contributions and that of Tuskegee, Taylor wrote:

Some of the methods and plans of the Institute of Technology [MIT] have been transplanted to the Tuskegee Institute and have flourished and grown there; if not the plans in full, certainly the spirit, in the love of doing things correctly, of putting logical ways of thinking into the humblest task, of studying surrounding conditions, of soil, of climate, of material and of using them to the best advantage in contributing to build up the immediate community in which the persons live, and in this way increasing the power and the grandeur of the nation."

Although Taylor could have worked for almost any university in the country, he remained at Tuskegee to help Washington teach the next generation of black students how to use their minds and hands improve their condition. Although he frankly acknowledged the sad plight of recently emancipated blacks, Taylor believed that when persuaded of the dignity of work and equipped with the necessary skills, former slaves could achieve economic independence and win the respect of a hostile white world.

But what did it mean for a black person to be conservative in the era of Jim Crow? What was it exactly those blacks had to conserve? As Kelly Miller noted in 1908:

No thoughtful Negro is satisfied with the present status of his race, whether viewed in its political, its civil or general aspect. He labors under an unfriendly public opinion, one which is being rapidly crystallized into a rigid caste system and enacted into unrighteous law. How can he be expected to contemplate such oppressive conditions with satisfaction and composure? ... Every consideration of enlightened self-respect impels him to unremitting protest, albeit the manner of protestation may be mild or pronounced, according to the dictates of prudence. Radical and conservative Negroes agree as to the end in view, but differ as to the most effective means of attaining it. The difference is not essentially one of principle or purpose, but point of view.[13]

Two things are immediately striking about these observations. One is that conditions for blacks in the legal realm have improved dramatically since Miller wrote those words. The law in both North and South has changed greatly to ensure, in writing, if not always in application, equal justice under the law regardless of color. Imperfections undoubtedly remain, and institutionalized racism is still all too common, but we cannot ignore the progress made. Similar success has been achieved in ensuring that

---

[13] Kelly Miller, *Radicals and Conservatives*, 1908.

blacks are treated more fairly in the marketplace. As a result of these reforms, the political and economic conditions for blacks have improved greatly, although much still remains to be accomplished.

This is where the other striking thing about Miller's observation arises. In the past half-century the radical black voice, the call for improvement through sweeping political change, has been predominant. Indeed, it has almost entirely shut out all other black voices. And as a result of its success, the radical black voice-often advocating greater governmental control over individuals, the economy, and private institutions-has been thought to be the voice of black America.

For more than a century, black American leaders have primarily looked to the political process to solve the problems of the black community. As a result, as Eugene Little noted in *Destiny* magazine (May-June 1993), "For many decades, blacks have been waiting: waiting for Congress to pass laws discouraging discrimination; waiting for society to design programs that will break the cycle of poverty; waiting for quick-fixes for urban decay; waiting for the 'experts' to come up with solutions. We are still waiting. The problem is not the lack of good intentions but the failure of government policies to help people take charge of their own lives. To perpetuate a system that clearly isn't working is foolish, unfair, wasteful, and even racist."

In the ongoing effort to use government to force social change and redistribute resources rather than concentrate on creating additional ones, the din of politics has drowned out the voice of black conservatism, the call for self-reliance, personal accomplishment, and a desire to contribute to society for the good of all and simply to reap the just rewards for one's achievements. This is a voice that is particularly needed at the present time. After all, what good can political and legal equality and economic freedom do for blacks if we are not poised to take advantage of these conditions? That is to say, if we are not prepared to step up to the plate educationally and through our personal efforts, no amount of economic and political concessions from the white majority can solve problems such as lack of initiative, mis-education, and dependency.

Despite the increasingly strong push for government intervention, conservative viewpoints continued to play a positive role in the black struggle for equality, prosperity, and dignity in the first half of the twentieth century. Zora Neal Hurston (1891-1960) was one of the most gifted writers to emerge from the Harlem Renaissance. She was recently described as a "conservative libertarian" by the *Wall Street Journal* in a review of two new books about her. Langston Hughes (1902-1967), Ralph Ellison (1914-1994), and Alain Lock (1885-1954), were also gifted conservative black writers from the Harlem Renaissance.

Today there are many impressive conservative black thinkers, though not all of them would accept the label. They include Dr. Walter Williams, chairman of the economics department of George Mason University; Dr. Thomas Sowell, the Rose and Milton Friedman Senior Fellow in Public Policy at the Hoover Institution; U.S. Supreme Court Justice Clarence Thomas; and Dr. Condoleezza Rice, U.S. Secretary of State. Several of these prominent black conservatives will be highlighted in more detail later in this book.

Conservative black academics and professionals are often maligned for their conservative views, and those who stay the course make up a small group. In the black community, the word "conservative" almost uniformly calls up disparaging and negative stereotypes. But conservatism today is not about protecting the status quo; thinkers and doers such as Sowell, Williams, Rice, and Thomas are calling for sweeping changes in government policy. Liberal policies - which now constitute the status quo - are not helping us achieve economic prosperity, academic excellence, healthy communities, or high moral standards. It is time for new voices to be raised, alternative solutions sought, and fresh ideas tried. Increasingly, these ideas come from conservative thinkers, building on intellectual foundations established in black America long ago.

Why "Black Conservatives" Are Less Prominent

A landmark in the modern emergence of black conservatism occurred in 1980 when The New Coalition for Economic and Social Change was founded following a major conference in San Francisco at the Fairmont Hotel. That meeting, known as the Fairmont Conference, was the first time since Booker T. Washington died in 1915 that a predominantly black group gathered to discuss conservative public policies. The speakers included Thomas Sowell, Clarence Thomas, Chuck Stone, Walter Williams, Edwin Meese III, and Milton Friedman. Proceedings from the conference were subsequently published by the sponsor organization, The Institute for

Contemporary Studies.[14]

At the Fairmont Conference, the New Coalition laid out an ambitious five point agenda:

1. To make blacks more economically independent;
2. To formulate a coherent strategy to deal with pathologies such as crime, poor health, unemployment, and miseducation that particularly affect people of color;
3. To publicize the fact that there is great diversity among blacks. We are not all poor or on welfare, nor do we all think alike;
4. To create new leaders and new alliances; and
5. To foster experts able to comment on a wide variety of issues, not just those commonly associated with "minority" concerns.

I became president of The New Coalition and "keeper of the flame" in 1993, after taking early retirement from the headquarters office of Sears, Roebuck, and Company. I have been working full-time on The New Coalition for the past fourteen years-without a salary, I might add. The New Coalition's mission is to cultivate effective multiethnic spokespersons, with conservative and libertarian views, and to help them gain access to forums where major public policies are being debated.

As I have discovered through my work at The New Coalition, over the past two decades conservative and libertarian ideas have gained an important foothold in the black community. Surveys show a majority of blacks consider themselves conservative, not liberal, on many issues. On some issues, such as school reform, blacks are to the right of whites. Yet self-acknowledged "black conservatives" are rarely seen or heard in public debates. One reason is obvious: conservatism in the black community is widely associated with white racism. Liberals, both black and white, work to create that perception in countless speeches and columns and in television ads during political campaigns. Some white conservatives do the same. The perception, largely left unchallenged, is widely accepted as reality. Unfortunately, conservatives have done little to challenge that perception.

There's also a clear double standard. A white liberal can say "I support

---

[14] *The Fairmont Papers, The Black Alternatives Conference, San Francisco, December 1980*, Institute for Contemporary Studies.

affirmative action" to a predominantly black audience, and he's met with a standing ovation. If a black public figure such as Colin Powell is for affirmative action, he is criticized by the liberal black leadership for not taking an even firmer stand, meaning one involving an even stronger role of government in our lives.

The double standard also exists among conservatives. A black conservative can give a talk before an audience of white conservatives and voice support for all the key ideas and policies of the conservative movement, but if he or she doesn't specifically denounce affirmative action the audience will express its disapproval. Opposing affirmative action is a litmus test imposed specifically on blacks by white conservatives.

The uses of the terms "affirmative action" and "conservative" in public debate actually have a lot in common, and they help explain why the words so fiercely divide both black and white communities. Affirmative action has been perceived by whites as being good for blacks and bad for whites. Conservatism has been perceived by blacks as being good for whites and bad for blacks. The logic is almost entirely the same on both sides-the only people we see on television or in newspapers who benefit from affirmative action are blacks, and the only beneficiaries of conservative policies we see are whites, and often wealthy and privileged whites at that.

Yet, whites have enjoyed and benefitted from affirmative action - and by this I mean favorable treatment not based on merit - more than any other group in America. It's perfectly natural and indeed unavoidable, because whites have far bigger and better social networks and more assets than blacks. When it comes to recommending someone or taking a risk when hiring or doing business, most of the time whites - like anybody else - choose people they know or who come recommended by someone they know. But how often do we see these white beneficiaries of affirmative action labeled this way in the news?

Similarly, blacks benefit the most from conservative policies. Tax cuts make a bigger difference to low-income families, entrepreneurs, and small investors than to the rich and secure. Deregulation lets small companies and people with new ideas compete with big corporations, whereas the latter often benefit from a paucity of new competitors entering the market due to the high cost of complying with complex regulations. Social Security privatization would also be a boon for blacks, who often die before they become eligible for Social Security benefits. But how often do we see the black beneficiaries of conservative policies labeled this way in the news?

A third reason black conservatives are rarely seen or heard from is the liberal bias of most foundations and corporate philanthropies. The vast majority of foundations, and nearly all of the biggest and best known foundations, simply refuse to fund conservative black spokespersons or organizations. Because hundreds of millions of dollars are given every year to advocacy organizations, this has a major impact on whose views are heard and whose are not. This is an insidious form of censorship that makes a mockery of the claims of many foundations and corporations to support genuine dialogue about the future of the black community.

Progress Being Made, Hope for the Future

Having said that, let me hasten to add that we are making real progress in communicating to whites that not all blacks seek government assistance at the expense of others' freedom, and to blacks that not all conservatives are racists. (Far from it!) Younger blacks are much more concerned about economic opportunity than older blacks are, and are more likely to be politically independent than wedded to the Democratic Party.

I received an email recently from a young lady who is a banker. She said, "I am 32 years old, married, with two children. I spent a long time in the Gulf War." She then recited all of the conservative principles we share. She said, "But I am not a Republican." And I said, "Welcome to the fold. We'll push the movement ahead if this is not about party." Adam Meyerson of the Heritage Foundation wrote some twenty years ago, "A substantial minority of African Americans are going to begin identifying with political conservatism rather than political liberalism." He predicted, however, that many of these conservative blacks would still belong to the Democratic Party.

The previously cited study from the Joint Center for Political Studies in Washington D.C. shows Meyerson was correct. The earthquake has started. I am hearing and feeling the tremors all the time. But the beneficiary of the change probably will not be the Republican Party, unless it changes its messages and practices dramatically. And this change is taking place largely without the support or even the awareness of foundations and philanthropies who pride themselves on supporting "black" charities and causes.

As Walter Williams has written, black people in the United States as a group have made the greatest progress, over some of the highest hurdles, in a shorter span of time than any other racial group in history. Black Americans are among the world's most famous and celebrated personalities - Oprah Winfrey, Michael Jordan, Bill Cosby, Tiger Woods, Clarence Thomas, the Williams sisters, to name just a few. The former chief officer of the world's mightiest military force and then U.S. Secretary of State, Colin Powell, is black. The current Secretary of State, Condoleezza Rice, is black. The president of McDonald's, the chairman of the board at Time-Warner AOL, and one Supreme Court associate justice are black. Blacks prove every day that they have what it takes to succeed in America.

More than three-quarters of America's black families now earn in the middle or upper income ranges. And consider this: 49 percent of black families owned their own homes in 2000 (up from 43 percent in 1990), and the average annual household income for blacks rose 27 percent (in constant dollars)-from $23,979 to $30,439-during that same period.[15] If blacks in the United States were a separate nation, it would be the thirteenth or fourteenth richest nation in the world.

Blacks accomplished this by "buying in with vigilance," according to Dr. Hardy Murphy, superintendent of the Evanston/Skokie school system, a suburb of Chicago. That means participating in the democratic and capitalist institutions of society, rather than standing outside them and complaining about their workings. It means taking advantage of the opportunities they present, instead of focusing on the increasingly small number of doors that have stayed shut. But it also means that we must remain vigilant about not losing sight of the values and choices that made us who we are today.

Few slaves or slave-owners would have predicted such achievements. However, we are not reminded of this impressive rising up of a race in school textbooks, in histories either academic or popular, or by popular commentators on race relations today, whether conservative or liberal. It's as if part of American history were being omitted, the part about how black Americans embraced the ideas of freedom and self-responsibility, and how when they were finally released from the chains of slavery and Jim Crow laws, most blacks eagerly and successfully took part in the American Dream.

This is the history and legacy that conservative blacks seek to conserve.

---

[15] *We the People: Blacks in the United States*, Census 2000 Special Reports, US Census Bureau, 2005.

Not memories of victimhood, losses, and injustice, but of rising above obstacles and accomplishing more than anyone thought possible. As Booker T. Washington wrote, "I have learned that success is to be measured, not so much by the position one has reached in life, as by the obstacles which he has overcome while trying to succeed."

As it is for anybody else, the road to success for blacks in America is through the acceptance of responsibility, cultural re-strengthening, regeneration of family structure and support, individual initiative and entrepreneurship, and education. These are things that government cannot create but can encourage. Conservative blacks, like all conservatives, believe that if government will only get out of the way, individuals and communities will step forward and unleash their great potential to contribute to society for the benefit of all.

Chapter 2

Booker T. Washington - The Consummate Conservative

Booker T. Washington (1856-1915) is the foremost exemplar of the black conservative vision. He arose from slavery to become one of the most famous and respected men of his time. His philosophy had three important themes: education, self-reliance, and entrepreneurship. Washington is known best for founding Tuskegee University, in Tuskegee Alabama, and for his lifelong advocacy of quality education, especially industrial education, for blacks of all ages.

Although many today have never heard of him, the Wizard of Tuskegee was, without doubt, the most significant and influential black leader of his time, and arguably of all time. He received honorary degrees from Harvard University and Dartmouth University, dined with the Queen of England, and was the first black person whose image appeared on a U.S. postage stamp and commemorative coin. President Eisenhower created a national monument to Booker T. Washington in 1956, and Washington was the first black inducted into the National Hall of Fame at New York University. Washington was the first black to have a battleship named after him, and Tuskegee University was the first black college to be visited by a U.S. President, William McKinley. In 1901, Washington was invited by President Theodore Roosevelt to dinner at the White House with his family, a historic event that aroused the ire of white supremacists across the nation.

When Booker T. Washington's papers were received at the Library of Congress in 1943 and 1945, the collection was massive. His papers included letters from Frederick Douglass, W. E. B. DuBois, Andrew Carnegie, John D. Rockefeller, President Theodore Roosevelt, Julius Rosenwald, President William Howard Taft, J. P. Morgan, and many others. Dr. Louis Harlan spent twenty-five years poring over the Washington papers collected in the Library of Congress before publishing his two-volume biography of Washington. Harlan won a Pulitzer Prize for his work, the first time a biography of a black had ever been so honored.

Washington's enormous stature was apparent to the academics of his day. William Dean Howells (1837-1920), widely regarded as the dean of American letters, described Washington as "a public man second to no other American in importance." Regarding Washington's famous speech at the Atlanta Exposition in 1895, Dr. Rayford W. Logan, head of history studies at Howard University, wrote, "Booker T. Washington's speech in Atlanta, Georgia, on September 18, 1895, was one of the most effective pieces of political oratory in the history of the United States. It deserves a place alongside that in which Patrick Henry proclaimed, 'Give me liberty, or give me death.'"[16] Logan added, "Structurally it was a model of organization, unity, and brevity." Clark Howell, editor of the *Atlanta Constitution* at the time, praised the speech as "one of the most notable speeches ever delivered to a Southern audience." Pulitzer Prize winner David Levering Lewis counted Washington's speech as "one of the most consequential pronouncements in American history."

When we recall that Washington began his life as a slave, his meteoric rise to greatness is even more remarkable. It is astounding that a man so widely respected and even revered by his contemporaries is now so thoroughly overlooked. What was it that made Booker T. Washington the central figure in American race relations at the dawn of the twentieth century? Indeed, why have historians labeled the years 1895 to 1915 "The years of Washington?" Answering these questions will help us understand the enduring appeal of black conservatism.

Washington's Social Philosophy

Booker T. Washington first leapt onto the national scene following the nationwide publication of his speech at the Atlanta Exposition in 1895. Perhaps it was fitting that 1895 was also the year of Frederick Douglass' death. Douglass, one of Washington's personal heroes, had been black America's spokesman and an ardent abolitionist for fifty years. Although Washington exercised a very different style of leadership, he inherited Douglass' firm belief in the strength and capability of his black brethren. When a white journalist had asked Douglass, "What do you blacks want

---

[16] Rayford W. Logan, *The Betrayal of the Negro from Rutherford B. Hayes to Woodrow Wilson*, 1897.

from white people?" Douglass famously responded, "Just leave us alone and we can take care of ourselves." Washington likewise believed former slaves could stand on their own feet and achieve prosperity in American society.

In the years leading up to 1895, Washington earned a solid reputation by founding and directing Tuskegee Institute, now Tuskegee University. While the federally established Freedman's Bureau had employed northern white men to establish and run black schools such as Fisk, Howard, and Hampton, Washington was the first black to head up such a school. As the principal of Tuskegee, teaching, fundraising, and administrating the school consumed the majority of his time. However, after his 1895 speech at the Atlanta Exposition - the first time a black man had ever shared the stage with southern whites - Washington assumed the mantle of black leadership from Douglass almost overnight. He became more than an educator; he became the hero and role model of his people.

Upon inheriting the mantle of leadership, Washington confronted the daunting challenge of transforming emancipated slaves into productive and prosperous citizens. The end of Reconstruction and the resurgence of a violent white supremacy movement further complicated his mission. After running Tuskegee for fourteen years, however, Washington had developed strong opinions about how blacks should pursue freedom and prosperity.

First and foremost, Washington advocated quality education for black children and adults. He understood that in the aftermath of slavery, freedmen needed schools that could teach them to read (something that was illegal under slavery) so they could develop the understanding and skills required of productive citizens. He founded the Tuskegee Institute in 1881, and for many years he quietly raised money from white philanthropists to fund new schools for blacks in the segregated South. In his autobiography, *Up from Slavery*, Washington noted that during the Reconstruction Period (1877 to 1878), "schools both day and night were filled to overflowing with people of all ages and conditions," some of them sixty to seventy years old. He observed, "The ambition to secure an education was most praiseworthy and encouraging."

This push towards education was done to promote Washington's second theme, self-reliance. Tuskegee University began as the Normal School in Tuskegee, and focused on training black men and women to become skilled at occupations such as construction and farming so that they could earn their way into the mainstream. Washington believed, as he wrote in *Up from*

Slavery in 1901, that "the actual sight of a first-class house that a Negro has built is ten times more potent than pages of discussion about a house that he ought to build, or perhaps could build."

A third Washington theme was entrepreneurship. Living at a time of intense racism and racial segregation, Washington encouraged thousands of black men and women to look at the need for goods and services in their communities as an opportunity to start their own businesses. In 1900, Washington founded the first black businessmen's association-the National Negro Business League (NNBL). He personally helped many black businesses get started by introducing black entrepreneurs to white investors.

One of these investors was Julius Rosenwald (1862-1932), chairman of the board of Sears, Roebuck, and Co. He gave away $100 million during his lifetime - half of which went to Southern black colleges and the building of five thousand schools for Southern black children. Rosenwald was so loyal to Washington that he was criticized within his own community for giving too much money to blacks. Washington was likewise criticized in his own community for being overly involved with whites. Still, a side benefit of their partnership was that it created a new dialogue between black and Jewish leadership that bore fruit during the civil rights movement. In 1905, a rabbi for the first time delivered the commencement address at Tuskegee. Four years later, a Jewish social worker would be one of three whites to meet in New York City and call for a conference with blacks on racial issues. The outgrowth of that conference was the National Association for the Advancement of Colored People.

Washington believed blacks would benefit most by building an economic foundation within the community, before focusing on politics as a route to the American dream. Given the failure of Reconstruction politics, in the Southern states in particular, Washington's approach seemed thoroughly logical. One of Washington's most famous statements was, "At the bottom of education, at the bottom of politics, at the bottom of religion, there must be for our race, as for all races ... economic independence."

In 1901, Washington published his autobiography, *Up from Slavery*, which became the best-selling book ever written by a black. It was eventually translated into seven languages and was as popular in Europe as it was in Africa. *Up from Slavery* was more than an autobiography, however; it was a ringing endorsement of Washington's major themes: education, self-help, and entrepreneurship.

Booker T. Washington committed his life to improving the lives of blacks wherever they were. He urged his race to do what was possible, instead of whining and pining over things outside their control at the time: In short, he recommended that we live well today, for the future will be better. In his time, Washington was Frederick Douglass, Martin Luther King Jr., and Nelson Mandela rolled into one.

Washington's Critics

Although Washington engaged the imagination and loyalty of blacks everywhere, especially in the South, he was not without critics. Washington's biggest antagonist during his lifetime was his one-time friend W. E. B. DuBois. Even though DuBois had requested a teaching position at Tuskegee several times - a request Washington repeatedly granted but DuBois then failed to accept when other career opportunities arose - DuBois eventually rejected Washington's social philosophy. In 1903, DuBois published his book *The Souls of Black Folks*, in which he criticized Washington and challenged him for leadership of American blacks. DuBois retracted his previous praise for Washington's speech at the Atlanta Exposition, dubbing it "The Atlanta Compromise." DuBois contended that without full political rights Washington's economic program would not help blacks achieve full equality with whites. DuBois grew increasingly frustrated at Washington's reluctance to take aggressive public stands against segregation and white-on-black violence.

DuBois also accused Washington of being opposed to higher education, specifically liberal arts education, for blacks. Washington, however, was a trustee of both Fisk and Howard Universities, and his daughter attended private schools in the East. Washington was not opposed to higher education in principle, but he did believe that the vast majority of his race ought to obtain a practical education that would lead to economic independence. It is important to remember that at this time relatively few Americans, black or white, attended college.

After the publication of *The Souls of Black Folk*, blacks essentially divided into two camps, one loyal to Washington and the other adhering to DuBois. Followers of the two men continued to vie with each other after Washington's untimely death in 1915. Subsequent black leaders - and importantly, the ones who were funded by white liberal philanthropists - overwhelmingly embraced DuBois' position.

For a century now, many historians discussing Dr. Booker T.

Washington have chosen to dismiss or vilify him and his views. Although there has been a steady increase in research on black leadership and historical scholarship, Washington has typically been overlooked. Dr. Robert Norrell, professor of history at the University of Tennessee, recently made the point that "DuBois' charges against Washington have been accorded more print space in history than Washington's response to it." DuBois' 1903 treatment of Washington in *The Souls of Black Folk* created an initial academic platform for criticism of the Wizard of Tuskegee, and the organization that supported DuBois, the NAACP, has played a major role in sustaining that distorted perspective.

Washington had to live with the criticism - which has echoed through time and is still heard today - that he was too modest in his demands on white society. It is the same criticism leveled against conservative blacks today. But after Washington's death in 1915 and when his personal papers were given to the Library of Congress, it was discovered that Washington was achieving tasks practically impossible for blacks to do at that time, such as hiring whites to spy on whites and hiring lawyers to fight the Jim Crow laws through the courts.

Washington could have proved to his critics at any time that he was not an "Uncle Tom," but he understood the strength of the opposition to his cause and the value of doing things quietly and without provoking additional opposition. He had a practical plan for his people, and accordingly he built institutions to support it - including his school in Tuskegee - which still stand today. His opponents were popular speakers and quick to mouth the popular leftist ideologies of the day, but they had no practical plan for actually improving people's lives.

While DuBois corrected the inaccuracies recorded in parts of his life story several times, he never owned up to the inaccuracies in his criticism of Washington. These inaccuracies have only recently been definitively refuted by the academic community.

Scholars Re-Appraise Washington's Legacy

A few scholars and historians are finally taking a fresh look at the legacy of Booker T. Washington. Even mainstream academia agrees that it is impossible to discuss black leadership at the turn of the twentieth century without acknowledging the twenty-year shadow of Washington. An essay in the November 28, 2003, *Chronicle of Higher Education* by Mark

Bauerlein, a professor of English at Emory University and a researcher at the National Endowment for the Arts, addressed Washington's influence. Bauerlein believes, "It is easy to envy Booker T. Washington, one of the most famous and respected men of his time, white or black." Washington had "access to the purse strings of Rockefeller and Carnegie," continues Bauerlein, "and enjoyed a wondrous intellectual prestige in a wildly racist world, and everyone but the most hardened white supremacist honored his person."

Proof of Rockefeller's respect for Washington can still be viewed at Riverside Church in Manhattan, built by Rockefeller. To the right side of Christ, high over the altar, are three statues: General Samuel Armstrong, founder of Hampton Institute (now a university); Abraham Lincoln; and Booker T. Washington. To show other examples of Washington's influence, Bauerlein's research points out that news reporters cited Washington's opinions weekly in the national press, and when he arrived in a city, reporters wanted his observations on the events of the day. Bauerlein doesn't dodge the controversy surrounding Washington's life and his conflict with DuBois. Bauerlein writes, "In our own time Washington stands as but a curiosity, the culpable antagonist of DuBois, Ida B. Wells-Barnett and the NAACP. To militants such as DuBois, and to us today, Washington's accommodationism is an abasement."

Then, Bauerlein offers a personal observation.

About a year ago, at an American studies conference, a distinguished scholar delivered a talk on the paradigm of the post-Reconstruction black intellectual, DuBois serving as model. In the discussion, when I asked how Washington fit into the scheme, the lecturer replied, 'I can pretty much do without Booker T.'" Bauerlein continues, "That characterization [from the lecturer] is too simple - not wrong, but too easy and extreme... . To appreciate Washington's tactics, we must return to the 1890s social scene, when lynch law was an open question... . It is easy, and mighty tempting, to judge figureheads of the past by standards of the present.

Dr. Harlan offers a similar assessment: "It is ironic that Booker T. Washington, who was the most powerful and influential black educator and leader of his time and perhaps of all times, should be the black whose claim to the title is most often dismissed by the lay public. Washington was a genuine black leader, with a substantial black following and with virtually the same long-range goals for black Americans as his rivals." As Thomas Sowell wrote in the December 1994 issue of *Forbes* magazine, the Booker-bashing was one of the most unfair hands dealt to any black leader in history.

Sowell has also defended Washington's speech at the Atlanta Exposition, arguing that rather than being a compromise it was a courageous piece of oratory. If we reflect on the circumstances in which Washington took the podium, we soon realize how delicate a situation Washington faced. "For a black man to be invited to address the distinguished audience at the Exposition was itself controversial," Sowell explained. "The South was a tinderbox of raw emotions over racial issues and more than a hundred blacks a year were being lynched. Voting rights, the right to serve in public office or on juries, and even basic personal security against violence were rights that Southern blacks once enjoyed ... [but] were now eroding."[17] That Washington was able to address a predominantly white audience, call for black advancement of any sort, and not start a riot is testament to his rhetorical genius.

Sowell is one of a growing number of scholars who are questioning the standard treatment of Washington since his death. "Booker T. Washington blazed forth as a black leader of character and strength," Sowell wrote. "Why is he today so often reviled as an 'Uncle Tom'?"

Washington's Vision Endures

The ideas of Booker T. Washington are just as relevant today as they were 100 years ago. When Washington was alive, there was intense opposition from whites to any effort to economically empower and educate the black community. Today, opposition is considerably less, and in fact there is much interest in reducing the "achievement gap" between white and black students, the cultural influences that encourage black boys and young men to drop out of school and become unemployable, and ways to increase the business creation rate for blacks. Blacks ought to capitalize on these favorable social conditions and move Washington's vision forward.

In considering the future of blacks, the central question is what kind of

---

[17] Thomas Sowell, "Up From Slavery," *Forbes Magazine*, 1994.

solutions we should be looking for: political, social, or economic? I argue for the economic solution, because a stronger economic foundation is the fastest route to first-class citizenship, and economic advancement can lead to political and social inclusion.

After Washington's untimely death in 1915, his vision of self-help and emphasis on economics were never fully accepted by the mainstream black elite or its white and largely liberal supporters. The emphasis for the past fifty years has been more on political and social integration rather than economic development. We now know, however, that political and social efforts without a strong economic foundation are of little value. We can no longer depend as much as we did in the past on the largesse of the federal government. The new call to arms must be for economic freedom and economic growth.

Washington knew that voting rights and marches are not the end of the struggle for equality. They are only the beginning. He understood that conservatism benefits blacks more than any other group by encouraging economic freedom, entrepreneurship, self-reliance, a useful education, moral strength, and religious faith. These are the things that blacks needed during Washington's time and need to be emphasized today if we are to take full advantage of the political freedom and civil rights we have won. The victories were meant to be the means to an end; they were not meant to be the end itself.

Booker T. Washington's vision can provide a true basis for finally and completely leveling the playing field for blacks, because of its attention to high expectations, education, and character. For example, blacks should aspire to become homeowners, instead of just moving into white neighborhoods. As Washington insisted, "The Negro must own his own land, milk his own cow, and hitch is own mule to his own wagon." What we need now is a strong economic foundation, not more political activism and protest. Economic freedom will include confronting racism wherever it still exists, but most of all it means that blacks should fight for a level playing field on which to achieve all that we are capable of accomplishing and contribute to society everything that we can. That will bring both economic rewards and true equality, as economic parity leads to social parity between blacks and whites. And that will be a winning formula for all.

The time seems right to discuss how Booker T. Washington's agenda can advance the black community and help it solve the problems that break up too many families and undermine its economic security. This "new" agenda will enable blacks to partake fully of the American Dream. Although Washington was truly a man of his times and knew his role was "to prepare and build," his lesson for us today is that we must have "character and strength to be equipped to compete."

Chapter 3

Education - The Key to the Conservative Vision

In the early years of the twenty-first century, there remains a persistently wide gap in educational achievement between black and white children. Ongoing national tests show that the average seventeen-year-old black student has about the same reading skills as the average thirteen-year-old white student.[18] In 2005 a study of student graduation rates from 1991 to 2002, funded by the Gates Foundation and conducted by the Manhattan Institute, calculated the percentage of all students that came through the public school system and received a high school diploma. The results were startling. The overall number was only 71 percent - and for blacks it was 56 percent, for Latinos 52 percent. The numbers are even worse for black males.[19] According to the Urban Institute, currently 56 percent of black females graduate from high school, and only 43 percent of black males.[20]

Unfortunately, these disturbing statistics have not aroused the black community to positive action to ensure that our young people stay in school and work hard to succeed academically. Many in the black community have come to believe that education is optional in light of high-profile blacks who have achieved riches and fame through sports or entertainment. For example, in 2005, "American Idol" winner Fantasia Barrino revealed that she could not read. The twenty-one-year-old star dropped out of high school and became an unwed mother at the age of seventeen. We can be happy for

---

[18] Jay P. Greene, *The Effect of Residential School Choice on Public High School Graduation Rates,* The Manhattan Institute, April 2005.

[19] Ibid.

[20] Christopher B. Swanson, *Who Graduates? Who Doesn't? A Statistical Portrait of Public High School Graduation, Class of 2001*, Urban Institute, 2004.

Barrino that her illiteracy has not kept her from productive employment and even fame. But that she is held up as an "idol" for her peers illustrates much that is wrong in black America today.

The black community simply does not take education seriously enough. There is no sense of outrage that so many inner-city schools completely fail to educate their students. With dropout rates of more than 50 percent and with much higher percentages of graduates unprepared to go on to college, today's public schools are the number one reason why far too many blacks have failed to enter the mainstream and achieve economic security.

Today, education is the most important function of state and local governments, especially with respect to the black community. We are slowly recognizing education as the number one civil rights issue among younger blacks, many of whom are fighting with older black leaders about educational choice as a viable strategy for addressing the problem of persistently failing public schools. Low-income parents in particular need better choices.

Equality, Not Just Integration, Is the Key

In 2004 the nation celebrated the fiftieth anniversary of *Brown v. Board of Education*, the landmark Supreme Court decision that abolished legal segregation in public schools. In May of 1954, Brown overturned the "separate but equal" doctrine established in the Court's 1896 *Plessy v. Ferguson* decision. Unfortunately, *Brown* got the law right but fell short on the implementation. Integration should have been a result, rather than a goal. Instead, integration became the sole end and even today has not been successfully implemented in most of the country's largest public school systems. While integrating schools has consumed the energies of a generation of black leaders and produced major backlash against the black community in many white communities, attempts to improve the public schools many black children attend was neglected.

The 1896 decision in *Plessy v. Ferguson* had determined that state laws mandating "separate but equal" accommodations for different groups of people were constitutional. The *Brown* decision overruled the "separate" part, but made no mention of making the accommodations "equal." Families that could afford to leave the cities moved to the suburbs en masse, leaving their poorer neighbors behind, and fifty years later public education remains unequal, with a persistently wide gap in educational achievement between black and white students.

By not giving higher priority to the term "equal," the Court ensured that the reality of the situation for most black students would be a state-sponsored, two-tiered system of public education. That said, *Brown* did effectively take the first step in dismantling legal segregation and became the framework of the modern civil rights era.

The *Brown* decision was a pivotal moment in American history, for Southern blacks in particular. The decision gets its name from a black family in Topeka, Kansas, who thought their young daughter Linda should be able to attend a public school closer to their home. Her application was denied because the school was for whites only, and the Supreme Court subsequently ruled public schools could not discriminate against children on the basis of race.

Mr. Brown's main concern, however, was not integrating the school; it was gaining the best possible education for his daughter. The white school was new and just seven blocks from his home. Brown himself had not been able to obtain a quality education in his youth, and he wanted his children to get a quality education - regardless of whether the school they attended was "black" or "white." The first lesson of Brown has to do with equal treatment for all citizens - not segregation. Of course, integration would have resulted if his children had been given equal access to the white school.

I was in the ninth grade on May 17, 1954, when the ruling was issued, and I remember it well. After growing up in the segregated society of Troy and Montgomery, Alabama, with separate "white" and "colored" water fountains in all the downtown stores, my fellow students and I paid close attention when the news on the radio reported the Court's decision. We were hopeful that the *Brown* decision would open the door for us to achieve a quality education, and we were eager to take advantage of such an opportunity.

Whenever I speak to black audiences today, the single message I try to communicate is that obtaining a quality education is the number one civil rights issue for the black community. Whereas integration is a task for government agencies to accomplish, obtaining a quality education is a collaborative effort among government, parents, and students. Today's parents and their children must seize the opportunities afforded them to gain an education. I fear that too many in our community believe that education is something passively received. The reality is that education must be pursued and opportunities seized. If the concern for failing schools could be raised to just half of the level of concern put forth over things such as presidential elections, more of our students would be finishing high school and going on to colleges and universities.

We can only wonder how different the last half-century would have been had the Brown decision focused less on the integration of blacks and whites and more on helping blacks achieve a quality education. The undeniable fact is that fifty years after Brown, black students still need to achieve much more.

Blacks could stand to relearn a lesson from Dr. Martin Luther King Jr. Before becoming a civil rights crusader, Dr. King earned a Ph.D., completing his studies by the age of twenty-six. The lesson is this: in order to fight for your dreams, you must be equipped to do battle. In fact, King himself said, "The discrimination of the future will not be based on race, but on education. Those without education will find no place in our highly sophisticated, technical society."[21] Since the 1960s, many blacks have been willing to jump into civil rights activism, but far fewer have been willing to pursue academic achievement and excellence.

Today, the opportunities to obtain a quality education abound. For example, every student in Illinois wanting to attend the University of Illinois who comes from a family with an income below the federal poverty level will receive grants to cover the full cost of a college education. In return, all that is asked is that the student work ten hours per week on campus. We must let our young people know about these opportunities and explain to them the vital importance of education.

Low Standards Bring Low Achievement

A prime example of the willingness to accept a poor, government-provided education system is the Ebonics controversy that erupted in the late 1990s. The Ku Klux Klan could not have come up with a better plan to impede the academic progress of young black children. Teaching Ebonics as a separate language, an idea popular among the political left, would create a nearly impenetrable barrier between poor black students and the dream of reaching

---

[21] Mr. Luther King Jr., *Why We Can't Wait* (New York, NY: Penguin Books, 1963)

the middle class. Crowning Ebonics as state policy would amount to a veiled admission of blacks' inability to master proper English, and would perpetuate the ghettoization of an entire generation. Why in the world would blacks rally behind a proposal the main outcome of which would be to lower educational expectations and leave their children unfit for competition in the economic marketplace?

In investigating the origin of Ebonics, scholars have traced constructions such as "I be" and "I ain't" and found their origin not in Africa but in England. Englishmen brought this dialect with them to America. This connection is further substantiated by the fact that many white Southerners speak in the same dialect. Choosing to call it Ebonics does not make it African.

As our study of Booker T. Washington should remind us, a good education has always been the key to advancement for African-Americans. Obtaining a good education is a step toward self-reliance and full citizenship. Over the last thirty years, however, we have lost sight of that goal, and we will continue to do so if we fall prey to the lure of masquerades such as Ebonics. My biggest concern about the entire controversy was that it was simply a diversion from the real problems of educating our youngsters. Education requires hard work and dedication to teaching, not complacency and excuses for failure based on junk sociology.

The idea of lowering standards is offensive to me. Martin Luther King Jr. did not walk into Boston University on a crutch when he received his doctorate in 1955, nor did W. E. B. DuBois when he received his degrees from Harvard. We do black students a disservice when we tell them that they cannot compete with white and Asian students.

Another major distraction from the essential quest for quality education is the glorification of athletes in the black community. Although it is undoubtedly rewarding to see blacks respected and elevated in the wider society, athletes should not be the primary role models for our children. The harsh truth is that a minuscule percentage of individuals will ever be able to achieve success in the elite world of professional sports. Opportunities for success in business, science, academia, and the professions, by contrast, are essentially unlimited. When our children fixate on the lucrative but nearly unattainable goal of athletic success, they lose sight of the real opportunities available to them.

In 1996, I witnessed a stark example of the wrongheadedness of our fixation on athletics. That year Farragut High School basketball star Ronnie

Fields saw his sports career destroyed as a result of an automobile accident. Fields was an extremely skilled basketball player, and he might have reached the professional National Basketball Association (NBA) but for the accident. He had averaged 33 points and 12 rebounds per game that season and twice had scored 51 points. He was one of the top five high school players in the country. Ronnie was the perfect West Side, inner-city, success story for sports writers.

After the accident, the media bemoaned the loss of Fields to Farragut's team and predicted that their dream of a state title was greatly diminished. What the media failed to cover was the grim reality that confronted Ronnie Fields after his accident. He had banked his future on his basketball skills, and now that they were gone, so were all of his hopes of upward mobility. Because Ronnie's academic problems had been winked at by teachers and coaches, he had repeatedly failed college entrance exams. There are thousands of high school students in the Chicago Public Schools (and in other major city systems) who continue to indulge in Ronnie's dream: the hope of making it to the NBA. Of those thousands of students, one or two might be selected, and the others will be left with a dream deferred - and a large number of them will be entirely unprepared for success in business, science, academia, or the professions.

What was lost in the Ronnie Fields story was the fact that sports careers can be fleeting. Academic achievement is not. I still remember when sports was an activity of amusement or a pastime, not a career path glamorized by the media. When teenagers can become star players and be drafted a year after high school to the NBA even though they have poor reading skills and cannot pass college entrance exams, we are taking basketball too seriously. When the coaches' priorities become game first, education second, parents must take the responsibility to ensure that their children's education comes first.

I'm not against sports at all. I simply want to see more African-American males succeed at college entrance exams. The number of headlines from sportswriters covering Ronnie Fields captured, at least for me, the best of times and the worst of times for young black Americans: the opportunities that sports can create and, conversely, the crisis that many young athletes face when they are unprepared for life after a career-ending injury or otherwise simply not being one of the rare few who make it to the professional level.

Student Performance Should Be Paramount

Several years ago the Chicago Public Schools system took center stage when the media reported that students were receiving passing grades while flunking tests. The city responded by closing the failing schools, and Mayor Daley eventually assumed control of the system. In response, droves of angry parents and community leaders descended on City Hall to protest the closing of failing neighborhood schools. Parents and community leaders were certainly right to be angry but their anger was misplaced. Rather than protesting the attempted reforms, they should have demanded more of them. They should have worried less about the closing of buildings and more about the shamefully poor education their children were receiving in those buildings. After all, what good is a high school diploma if future employers discover you can't read?

Another example of our frequently misplaced priorities occurred in March 2006 when Chicago suffered a controversy over the honorary naming of a city street after former Black Panther Fred Hampton. I was surprised that one little street on the west side of Chicago could become such a big controversy. It's a shame we can't get communities this upset about how poorly schools are educating our kids.

Unfortunately, many parents do not realize how badly the public school system has failed their children. For example, according to the National Assessment of Educational Progress for 2005, an astounding 70 percent of Illinois fourth-graders couldn't read at levels the government considers proficient, and 68 percent weren't proficient in math. And the problem didn't affect poor kids only. In Chicago, 32 percent of students who were not eligible for the school lunch program, which targets needy families, still failed to read at basic levels. So why aren't parents protesting that their children aren't being taught to read? In many cases, it's because they actually don't know that the institutions they are marching to defend have failed their children so badly.

Money Is Not the Answer

To distract parents from the real problem, politicians and the education establishment continuously complain about an entirely fictitious lack of money and demand more. The Black Caucuses in state legislatures, teachers unions, and self-proclaimed "civil rights organizations" continuously demand that governors and legislatures come up with new plans to boost funding for schools.

I hope these parents' justifiable anger will not continue to make them pawns for the ongoing war waged by teachers unions and the Black Caucus against taxpayers and those who would actually do something to improve our children's education by breaking the public schools' stranglehold. Unions are for teachers, and schools are for students. The closing of a failing school is reform. Parents' highest priority should be education reform. Where is the uproar over the failure of schools to educate our students? We talk about how many blacks are in jail and how much it costs to keep them there. Quality education is what's needed to improve that situation.

The legacy of education in the black community is a long one. When blacks came to this country, as free men or slaves, they quickly realized that education represented, among many things, freedom and access to the American dream. Although the education made available to them was unequal, blacks still managed to make progress. Yet more than fifty years after the Supreme Court's *Brown v. Board of Education* decision, blacks are still tragically behind in obtaining a quality education that would enable them to be economically independent and culturally successful. Quality and results, not more dollars for a sclerotic, complacent educational bureaucracy, are what black Americans should be pressing for.

Inkling of Hope

Although the educational system is clearly in trouble, there are some encouraging signs that parents are starting to get more involved. A recent survey by Black Entertainment Television and CBS found that 61 percent of black adults polled want their children to go to college and graduate school. Unfortunately, the minority communities and all of society pay the price for poor academic practices and outcomes in K-12 education. All businesses, particularly black and Latino businesses in the inner city, have a stake in the current public school reform debate, for economic growth depends not just on higher reading and math test scores but on having more efficient employees.

There are many positive examples of the use of best practices throughout the Chicago Public Schools system. Effective leadership at the school board as well as in the local school councils has made a difference in recent years. And social promotions, which resulted in unprepared students graduating from high schools, appear to have been curtailed. However, there still needs to be stiffer competition between failing schools and those that do a better job.

One answer might be this: if after three years a school has not been removed from the state's "watch list," allow students to choose another school and let state funds follow the child. Herbert J. Walberg, a research professor of education and psychology at the University of Illinois, notes, "The biggest federal education program, Title 1 for impoverished students, cost more than $100 billion over the past 25 years." Despite the cost, he observes, elementary and secondary education performance has not significantly improved.

Choice Is The Key

At the Fairmont Conference in San Francisco in 1980, economist Milton Friedman told the group gathered that blacks "have had bad schooling because it is provided by the government, and because the poor people of this country have no other alternative."[22] Friedman told the group that other "ethnic groups succeeded by taking advantage of the opportunities that the private market offered them." Himself a Jew, he said "the Jews certainly did not succeed because they were getting special government privileges. The Japanese did not succeed on that ground. The Chinese did not succeed on that ground. They all succeeded by taking advantage of the opportunities that the private market offered them. And I think this is a subject that is gaining widespread interest."

The concept of school vouchers has been widespread for fifty years now but has yet to be seriously implemented at the state level. The state of Utah passed such a law in early 2007, but it is under challenge, and the vouchers don't approach the full cost of tuition, especially for families with non-poverty incomes (And remember, three quarters of black families in the U.S. have middle or upper incomes). Nonetheless, passage of the Utah law is a significant event and a huge step in the right direction. The idea of a voucher is fairly simple: parents receive a stipend from the state that they can use to pay tuition at the school of their choice. Parents control the flow

---

[22] Milton Friedman, "Government is the Problem," in *The Fairmont Papers: Black Alternatives Conference, San Francisco, December 1980*, Institute for Contemporary Studies, 1981.

of money, rather than school district bureaucracies. Because parents have options, they can "vote with their feet" and encourage schools to compete for their money.

If competition raises the level of every other good and service, why should education be any different? In fact, competition works quite well in the arena of higher education, where federal loans allow students to choose the school that will receive their money. The book *Education and Capitalism*, written by Herbert Walberg and Joseph Bast and published by the Hoover Institution in 2003, is a masterful argument for school choice at the elementary and high school level. Given the disastrously poor service they have received from public schools nationwide, blacks should use their skills in political activism, honed through years of agitating for withheld rights, to urge legislators for expanded school choice programs.

This is urgent. We cannot keep asking the next generation to sacrifice its future on the altar of our politics. We're never going to make everyone happy - someone will always oppose reforming even the worst schools. But it's time our elected officials stop worrying about whether everyone agrees, and give parents the freedom to move their kids to another school.

Too many public schools are increasingly run for the benefit of some adults they employ and the contractors they pay, not the children who fill their classrooms. The lie that undergirds the enemies of vouchers is that "vouchers will destroy the public system." That's sheer nonsense and merely serves as a talking point for union leaders and politicians. Some public schools, suburban and city, are doing well and do not require dramatic changes. But we African-Americans have to ask some serious questions. What's wrong with us? We are ready to march for everything, but why do we make so little effort to protest the black education gap? We have firm results from a two-year study that included New York City, Washington, and Dayton, Ohio, which found that school vouchers improved the performance of black students enrolled in underperforming city schools.[23] Neither conservatives nor Republicans conducted the study - it was done by the liberal Brookings Institute and Harvard University. If we are willing to march to protest the execution of violent criminals, surely we could march to expand and implement elsewhere the remarkably successful school voucher programs that have been instituted in these and other

---

[23] William G. Howell and Paul E. Peterson, *The Education Gap: Vouchers and Urban Schools, Revised Edition*, The Brookings Institute, 2006.

American cities!

Opinion polls show support for vouchers runs as high as 80 percent in the African-American community. Years ago I organized the first meeting for black parents to explain the voucher system. The event was appropriately held at Milton Friedman's longtime home, the University of Chicago. Although I understand that many in the African-American community have been told that they are indebted to the public school system for what it has accomplished in the past, the reality is that it has not kept pace with the educational demands of today. The solution is vouchers, and we should be at least as passionate in support of this fundamental change as we are about any other issue of our time.

Children Wither While Leaders Dither

Unfortunately, the current black leadership strongly opposes vouchers. Hence, I believe that if blacks are ever to achieve quality education, it will have to happen outside the bounds of the traditional civil rights leadership. Mainstream leaders such as Jesse Jackson and Al Sharpton have demonstrated that academic achievement for black children is not their priority.

This point came home to me during the explosive controversy over the failure of the East St. Louis School System. Three hundred miles southwest of Chicago, black schoolchildren in East St. Louis in the late 1990s - and sadly, still today - were the victims of one of the biggest educational travesties in America, but the great left-liberal black leaders were nowhere to be found. The crisis involved District 189 in East St. Louis, a public school district serving 12,000 students. The district was 99 percent black. It had been called "the worst in the nation." The *St. Louis Post-Dispatch* reported, "more than 75 percent of the high school students can't meet minimum state standards for reading, math, writing and science. Half the male students had dropped out by the 10th grade."

A former instructor in one of the district schools pleaded guilty to embezzling $90,000 and admitted having sex with female students. Toilets were broken, and in some cases there was no soap or toilet paper in the restrooms. At one point the police picked up a prostitute and discovered that she was an East St. Louis substitute teacher.

So, where was our black leadership, including the Rev. Jesse Jackson? He has rallied the troops over much smaller offenses, but apparently he didn't believe that the failure of the East St. Louis public school system merited a response. It was probably because the East St. Louis school crisis was not the typical victimization story - in this case, blacks were abusing blacks through shameless neglect or outright corruption.

Anita Hicks, mother of nine-year-old twins, sued the system, charging that the East St. Louis School District was failing to teach its children and that Illinois had a constitutional responsibility to take over the system. None of Illinois' black leaders took up her cause. None of the state's civil rights or liberal advocacy groups backed her. Of course the teachers union opposed the lawsuit.

Has black-on-black abuse become so commonplace that it's considered business as usual? Or is it a far touchier issue for civil rights leaders to solve the problem and assign blame when a situation is not a black-vs.-white conflict?

Perhaps a problem is only acceptable to deal with when one of the few white students in the system calls one of the black students the "N" word. Only then might we see a march on East St. Louis. But it is unlikely that we will see a more constructive debate over something that would really help solve problems like the one in District 189: parental choice and responsibility instituted through a school voucher system.

Within the black community, we continue to talk about our failing public school system, but have done nothing about it other than to blame others for it. We must at least develop an attitude that there is something we can do, and then do it.

It's not a question of integration or affirmative action. I graduated from an all-segregated public system in Alabama that worked. We hear a lot about the Rev. Martin Luther King's dream, and Anita Hicks has a simple dream too: that her son and daughter receive a quality education in East St. Louis. For now, it seems to be an impossible dream, and all too few in black America seem to care.

Fighting the Achievement Gap

As the East St. Louis example demonstrates, blacks have to take responsibility for the schools their taxes pay for, and that means forcing change where it is needed. Problems in suburban schools became apparent in the Chicago area in 2003, becoming a major topic of concern with many parents of the Evanston-Skokie (suburban Illinois) District 65 school system. Some parents and taxpayers in this small, affluent suburb on Lake Michigan, just north of Chicago, were wondering just how much - if at all - black students have really benefitted from the desegregation policies adopted more than four decades ago. A major concern was the gap in test scores between black and white students.

In September 2003, The New Coalition for Economic and Social Change co-hosted with Northern Trust Bank a "town hall" evening reception and meeting to discuss this serious and emotional community topic. An overflow crowd of fifty came to hear remarks by Dr. Hardy Murphy, superintendent of Evanston-Skokie District 65. Murphy, who is black, was appointed superintendent of the Evanston-Skokie district in June 1999. Prior to that appointment, he was the associate superintendent of the Fort Worth (Texas) Independent School District, a K-12 district with 113 schools. In Evanston, Murphy serves a public elementary and middle school district of sixteen schools and approximately 7,000 students.

In each of the sixteen schools, the district has a guideline that limits numbers for any one racial or ethnic group to no more than 60 percent of total student enrollment. While most parents appreciate the goal of integrated schools, Murphy said, serious questions arise when a school serves a neighborhood of basically one racial or ethnic group.

In the mid-1960s, busing was thought to be the solution to the problem of unequal school quality, but most observers today realize it is not the panacea people once thought it to be. Evanston-Skokie figures show that black students are bused more often than white students. Some parents worry that the students who are bused are not able to participate in after-school programs for students who need additional help. Black students in the district are trailing their white counterparts on standardized test scores.

"The system has served white parents very well," said Murphy. "But when you talk to black parents, you learn they don't share that perspective." There is racial tension in the district, said Murphy, of a kind not usually associated with affluent school districts, especially where the superintendent is black and the mayor, who is highly popular, is also black. To begin addressing the tension, Murphy set up a new partnership with Evanston-based Northwestern University to improve teaching and learning in the district's schools. Murphy believes that the partnership, along with other efforts he has initiated to get parents, teachers, and students working more closely with each other, will reduce the gap in test scores. The cause for optimism is that Murphy's effort is aimed directly at improving the district's educational quality and student achievement, rather than integration for the sake of integration.

Working Educational Miracles

One of the most encouraging examples of what black students can accomplish when they are not shackled by low expectations and public school bureaucracy is in the work of Marva Collins. I first met Mrs. Collins in 1984. As a corporate executive and community activist, I was cosponsor of a conference on educational choice aimed at black parents, and Collins was my keynote luncheon speaker. Little did I know at the time that a decade later I would join her board of directors, leave the corporate world, and found The New Coalition for Economic and Social Change.

Marva N. Collins is a nationally known educator and founder of two successful private schools located in Chicago and Milwaukee. She grew up in Atmore, Alabama, during the period of segregation. Black children were not allowed to use the public library, and their schools were given only a small collection of books. But Marva's father, a successful businessman, helped develop her strong desire for learning, achievement, and independence.

After graduating from Clark College in Atlanta, Georgia, Marva Collins taught school in Alabama for two years. She then moved to Chicago, where she taught in the public school system for fourteen years. Her experiences in that system, and her dissatisfaction with the education her children were receiving in prestigious private schools, convinced Collins to open her own school on the second floor of her home. She began her program in 1975 with $5,000-her entire pension. Six children were enrolled: her own two youngest children and four neighborhood youngsters. Thus the Westside Preparatory School, located in Chicago's Garfield Park neighborhood, was born.

From her very first year, Collins taught children labeled "unteachable" by other schools. By the end of the year, their scores had increased at least five grade levels, proving that the children were anything but "unteachable." Collins soon gained a reputation for producing dramatic results in short periods of time. Her success led to profiles in *Time* and *Newsweek* and television appearances on "60 Minutes" and "Good Morning, America." CBS profiled her life in a 1981 television movie, "The

Marva Collins Story."

In a 1995 book titled *The Bell Curve*, Charles Murray questioned Collins' success, saying her work would have no lasting effect on the children. "60 Minutes," which had showcased 33 of Collins' young students in 1979, returned to Westside Preparatory School in 1995 to find out how those 33 students had fared. Statistically, given the demographics of her class, one student would have been dead, two in jail and five on welfare. All 33 students, however, were thriving in 1995, some in college and others working in successful careers. A majority of her former students had actually chosen careers in teaching.

At the end of 1996, 109 Chicago-area schools were placed on academic probation. Collins chose to help the three lowest-achieving schools in the worst Chicago neighborhoods and with the lowest levels of parental involvement. Two schools decided to implement the Marva Collins' Methodology, while one declined. After just four months, the schools adopting Collins' approach experienced test score improvements of more than 85 percent. The other school showed score improvements of just 10 percent.

Collins has received more than forty honorary doctoral degrees, including degrees from Dartmouth and Notre Dame. She has trained Fortune 500 executives, other business people, and more than 100,000 teachers, principals, and administrators worldwide. She has written and published several books on education and teaching. Collins now lectures internationally, and her daughter, Cynthia, is the headmistress of The Marva Collins Preparatory School in Chicago. Collins's son Patrick conducts teacher-training seminars in Chicago and around the country.

Education Is Key

In today's information age, education is the dividing line between those who thrive and those who merely survive. Although blacks are no longer barred from public schools and segregation is now against the law, blacks continue to underachieve academically. We have tried in vain for forty years to improve the public education system that fails our students so miserably in cities all across America. The time has come for blacks to stand up and demand a change of policy. The one skill that we have developed, perhaps better than any other group, is the skill of political agitation. To date, however, we have not collectively used our political strength to demand lasting school reform in the form of school choice.

Milton Friedman pointed out over forty years ago that the problem with public education is not lack of funds, low regard for teachers, dilapidated buildings, or even low parental involvement. The fundamental problem is that public education is provided by the government. The beauty of school choice is that the government ensures each child a quality education without bureaucratically monopolizing the delivery of the education. This principle works extremely well in other spheres of life. For example, food stamps, higher education grants and loans, Medicare, and Medicaid are all instances in which the government provides the money but private parties provide the service. It is incredible that we have not yet seriously attempted vouchers on a statewide or nationwide level for K-12 education.

At some point the black community will grow tired of receiving inferior education, and my hope is that when this happens we will once again take to the streets to pursue the most significant civil rights issue of our time, educational freedom. Excellent education at the elementary and secondary levels will enable blacks to compete at the undergraduate and graduate levels without the demeaning affirmative action programs that perpetuate the myth of black inferiority. An increase in educational attainment will then empower more blacks to achieve the middle class life that has long been known as "The American Dream."

Chapter 4

Entrepreneurship - Creating Wealth and Opportunity

In our centuries-long quest for full civil rights, it is now high time to pursue the economic solution. Booker T. Washington urged the economic solution, but the desire for full political rights trumped his emphasis on economic development, perhaps understandably. A strong economic foundation, what might be called a middle class lifestyle, is the fastest route to first-class citizenship and full enjoyment of our hard-won political rights, as Washington often reminded his students at Tuskegee. Blacks in the United States have not yet achieved the complete economic independence Washington worked towards. Unemployment, underemployment, and welfare dependency still afflict us as a people.

History demonstrates that Carter Woodson was correct in his 1933 publication, The *Mis-education of the Negro*, when he declared, "It does not matter who is in power or what revolutionary forces take over the government: those who have not learned to do for themselves and have to depend solely on others never obtain any more rights or privileges in the end than they had in the beginning."[24] As long as a large percentage of blacks in America are dependent on the government for their daily bread, full emancipation will remain a distant dream.

This lesson came home to me when in 2006 a *Chicago Sun-Times* article appeared claiming, "Early Deaths Tied to Lack of Grocery Stores." The story left the impression that poor health in the black community was somehow a simple matter of "access" to grocery stores, and it implied that blacks ought to protest and petition the government to deal with the situation. But when we asked why there were so few grocery stores in black neighborhoods the answer was troubling. The lack of entrepreneurial values in black communities had made locally owned grocers unheard of, and the

---

[24] Carter G. Woodson, *The Mis-Education of the American Negro* (Associated Publishers, 1933).

communities' very real crime problems had scared off corporate chains. And when a big chain such as Wal-Mart did want to come in (yes, Wal-Mart sells food too), various members of the Chicago City Council and the labor unions attempted to keep it from happening. As a result, the black community was without access to basic grocery services and came limping to government for help.

Prior to Woodson, at the turn of the century, the emphasis in the black community was on economics as the most feasible route for advancement. But since then the emphasis has been more on political rights and social integration rather than economic development. How did we get so sidetracked? The political and social framework is in place. We must now build and own our own homes, instead of just moving into the neighborhood and paying rent. We need to start our own businesses so that we will not be at the mercy of corporate outsourcing and downsizing. We must avoid the consumer debt so endemic to American society today by living frugally, saving money, and investing wisely. If we revive the vision of Booker T. Washington and pursue economic independence, we may finally achieve a measure of self-determination and prosperity that has thus far eluded us.

Investing in the Future

Dependency on government is a dangerous trap. One of the often overlooked ways that blacks could set about pursuing economic independence would be by supporting personal savings accounts as an alternative to the current Social Security system. Social Security takes control out of the hands of the individual and places the burden on the government to provide for our retirement. Why are we so in love with a system that takes our money for the duration of our working lives and offers virtually no rate of return? I believe that fear of personal financial responsibility keeps us dependent upon the federal government.

In 2005, I went on National Public Radio to debate David Certner, director of federal affairs for the American Association of Retired Persons (AARP), the seniors advocacy group. The topic was Social Security reform. I spoke in favor of setting up individual, private accounts that would safely invest in the economy and provide a much higher return than Social Security currently does, which AARP opposes. Setting the record straight on Social Security rates of return and its effect on blacks is long overdue.

Blacks have a huge stake in this debate. A 2004 study by AARP presented to the Congressional Black Caucus, showed that 50 percent of black Americans age 65 or older depend on Social Security for 90 percent or more of their income.[25] For these folks, Social Security is nearly their sole source of retirement income. This dependence leads most black leaders to say, "Social Security is critical to our community; don't change it." AARP echoes their concerns when it says, "Personal saving and investment should be done in addition to Social Security, not in place of it."

But change will be essential if we want to save the concept of Social Security, and it is definitely needed. President Bush has repeatedly focused on the year 2018 instead of 2042 because that's when benefits are projected to exceed revenues from payroll taxes. When Social Security was created in 1935, the normal retirement age was 65, and the average life expectancy for white males was 67 years. This meant that a worker would be paying into the system for over forty years but collecting on average just two years' worth of benefits. Back then, there were 30 to 35 workers paying Social Security taxes for each person receiving benefits. The tax rate for employees was one percent. In 1960, there were five workers for every Social Security beneficiary. Today, there are slightly more than three. In thirty years, there will be only two. That means fewer tax-paying workers to support more benefit-receiving retirees.

Does Social Security cheat black Americans? The short answer is yes! In a 1998, report, the Heritage Foundation showed that black Americans generally receive a much smaller return on their "investment" in Social Security taxes than whites.[26] The report indicated that a major factor in black Americans' poor returns from Society Security is the sad fact that so many black workers die before they can receive significant benefits.

As this debate mushrooms, blacks are being targeted by both sides. It is interesting that young black voters, who will be affected most significantly by policy decisions, have not yet made their voices heard in the debate. The major flaw in the existing system is that although it provides a measure of security for retirees, the accumulated benefit cannot

---

[25] Ke Bin Wu, "African Americans Age 65 and Older: Their Sources of Income," *AARP Public Policy Institute*, 2004.

[26] Daniel J. Mitchell, "Social Security Trust Fund Report Shows Need for Reform," *The Heritage Foundation,* 1998.

be passed on to provide financial security for one's children and grandchildren. The key to retirement security and upward social mobility is wealth creation.

Blacks would be right to oppose private Social Security accounts if it were true that they would cause reductions in benefits for current beneficiaries and in programs for the poor. But this does not have to be the case. Current retirees and those about to retire can be guaranteed their full benefits. Middle-aged people can be given a choice of whether to join a new system with private accounts or stay with the current program. And young people will get a vastly better deal than they would from the current system.

Working with the Churches

In order to shed dependency on government and embrace economic independence, blacks need to hear how conservative political solutions work to their advantage. Given that the church is a powerful force in black Americans' lives, and the huge influence of the social ideas promulgated there, economic education for the clergy, aimed at helping them work more effectively with both the government and the private sector, is truly an idea whose time has come. A first-of-its-kind conference, held in 1996 at the Federal Reserve Bank of Chicago, was an important first step in that direction. Efforts in this direction can spur an increase in low and middle-income mortgage and business lending handled through churches.

This half-day conference, where I was a participant, was not a usual Fed event. The discussion was not about the flow of money and credit through the economy. It was not aimed at corporate America. That particular morning, Federal Reserve President Michael Moskow and John Skorburg, chairman of a group called Economic Education for Clergy, made presentations to about seventy-five members of the Chicago clergy and other community activists. The meeting was about how economic relationships could be developed to help rebuild depressed areas of Chicago. The importance of this meeting to the black clergy in particular is twofold. First, since the days of slavery the black church has been the community rock upon which successful organizations built their foundations.

Second, the black community is suffering under a moral and family crisis that is not being addressed by government, politics, the private sector, or public schools. Only the church has the experience, expertise, and moral authority to accept this challenge. Many of our churches, small and large, are run by men and women who are trained only in theology and have never heard of Adam Smith. Yet they are a group ready to carry forth the vision of self-reliance.

One surprise during the presentation was that questions regarding racial discrimination led to lively discussion. There is still a wide gap between minorities seeking loans and lenders who will accommodate them. Many times, such meetings turn into social chaos, but not this time. One of the social-change missions of many churches and synagogues since the 1990s has been a direct emphasis on urban economic development. Since civil rights organizations and political leaders are fumbling badly in terms of community leadership, religious leadership is reasserting its authority over moral and economic issues. For the first time since the 1960s, they are in charge of an agenda beyond civil rights. The new challenge includes reestablishing moral principles and building an economic foundation within each community.

Redefining Minority Business in a Changing Economy

To help lay the foundations for greater economic independence for black Americans, Booker T. Washington established the National Negro Business League in 1900 and encouraged blacks to start small businesses to meet the ever-present demand for goods and services in their communities. But who speaks for minority businesses a hundred years later? One organization that works to advance minority businesses is the National Minority Supplier Development Council (NMSDC), a twenty-seven-year-old organization that provides a direct link between corporate America and minority-owned businesses. It has more than 3,500 corporate members and more than 15,000 minority businesses working through thirty-nine regional councils across the country.

Harriet Michel, a public policy expert and president of NMSDC, in a 2000 *Wall Street Journal* interview, explained that the number one problem facing minority-owned businesses was a lack of access to capital needed to grow.[27] She announced that it is time to move beyond the present definition

---

[27] Harriet Michel, "Minority Firms May Decide To Redefine Themselves," *The Wall Street Journal*, November 4, 1998.

of a minority business. Since the 1960s, the standard federal definition of a minority business has been 51 percent ownership by a minority.

Ms. Michel wants to expand the definition and add a category called the "growth initiative." The proposal was designed to provide minority businesses with the potential for substantial growth and the ability to access equity capital, while retaining management control. When word of the proposed change began to circulate, an emotional debate ensued. Fortunately, Ms. Michel won the contest. Under the group's new guidelines, minorities must continue to control the voting stock and a majority of the seats on the board of directors, but minorities do not need to control 51 percent of the equity stock. As long as 31 percent of the equity stock is owned by minorities the company still qualifies as an MBE. This change allowed Minority Business Enterprises (MBEs) to raise money from large institutional investors while retaining their classification as an MBE.

Many minority-owned businesses have taken advantage of Ms. Michel's innovation to raise capital from large investment companies and expand their businesses. The NMSDC still serves an important role in connecting these MBEs with other companies that want to do business with minorities. I agree with Ms. Michel's idea and her vision. A leader's role should be to find solutions that will grow his or her organization and give better service to its customers. The real question is why would MBEs want to limit their sources of capital? This idea will create real progress if institutional investors are interested in a win-win relationship with minority businesses.

The Power of the (Black) Press

Another institution that can do more to strengthen black Americans is the black press. One of the most successful stories of black enterprise of all time is that of the *Chicago Defender*, the black daily newspaper for the Windy City. I have been an editorial board member for several years now and continue to write regular columns for the paper. I believe the inspirational story of Robert Sengstacke Abbot, founder and original owner of the *Defender*, should be told to every black youth thinking about starting a business.

On May 5, 1905, Robert Sengstacke Abbott (1870-1940) was standing on South Side street corners selling a four-page newspaper-handbills filled with local news, which he called the *Chicago Defender*. As the years went by the new Chicago paper expanded to thirty-two pages, and Abbott became one of the first African American millionaires by succeeding against the odds in journalism. His journey began as a student from the state of Georgia who graduated from Hampton Institute with a degree in printing, and moved to Chicago in 1897. He worked at odd jobs while earning a law degree at Kent College of Law. Due to racial discrimination and prejudice, however, it was virtually impossible for him to earn a living as a printer or as a lawyer.

Yet, being a young man who made no excuses nor fell prey to victimization, he also saw a need for informing African Americans in Chicago about what was happening that was affecting their lives. The life lesson in Robert Sengstacke Abbott's story is that life includes closed doors. The challenge is to find the open doors, for success usually follows.

While Abbott was a student at Hampton he had the opportunity to study under the first black to teach black Americans and Native Americans, Booker T. Washington. Although Washington was twelve years Abbott's senior, the teacher and student remained friends until Washington's untimely death at age 59 in 1915. An example of their relationship is shown in the following letter, dated December 19, 1913, marked personal and confidential, which is at the Library of Congress:

> In addition to what I said to you yesterday ... I am glad to see that your paper is taking this sensible view.... . Another thing we must learn sooner or later, and that is, that no matter how much a certain type of white people may promise to do for us in the way of securing "rights," in the last analysis, we have got to help ourselves.

That statement from Washington in 1913 is just as relevant today. The *Defender* continues to inform black Americans. Through the years, the *Chicago Defender* has been an institution in the community that has nurtured and informed its readers. The *Defender*, the largest daily black newspaper in the country, continues to strive to be the newspaper Robert S. Abbott knew it could become.

In the late 1990s the late John H. Sengstacke, Robert S. Abbot's heir, died, and his family began addressing how to maintain the *Chicago Defender*. At the time this written, the *Defender* is still in transition. There are large economic and social issues surrounding the paper that have not been honestly discussed. Put simply, the *Defender* needs to update its editorial mission to better serve African-American readers in Chicago if it is to survive. Chicago has the second-largest black population among U.S. cities and is home to the largest black middle class. Yet the *Chicago Defender* has not kept pace. Its circulation has fallen to between 16,000 and 19,000, down from more than 50,000 in the 1950s.

Why does Atlanta, which ranks seventh in black population, have a weekly black newspaper that outsells Chicago's? It raises the question of whether the *Defender*, with ninety-two years of history in Chicago, is still appealing to its core audience. I have always purchased the *Defender* because it supposedly focuses on the black community. Over time, however, the paper's ability to tap into the changing economic, social, and political views of black Chicago has diminished.

In order to flourish, the *Defender's* focus must extend beyond the South and West sides of the city, where most blacks in Chicago have traditionally lived. Readers and potential readers are now living all over the city and surrounding suburbs. The black community is not monolithic. And that statement applies to politics and social values as well. The *Defender* should greatly reduce the number of stories that perpetuate victimization and remove all race-baiting from its pages.

Liberal Economic Policies Harm Black Communities

The editorial policies of the *Chicago Defender* exemplify the lack of diversity of opinion allowed black Americans by mainstream media outlets. If blacks are ever to achieve the type of economic success envisioned by Booker T. Washington, we will have to become savvier about basic economic principles. Time and again, blacks have supported liberal economic policies that end up stripping away jobs and harming our communities. The recent flap in Chicago over the so-called big-box ordinance is a perfect example of such economic confusion.

The big-box ordinance passed in July 2006 by the Chicago City Council and vetoed by Mayor Richard M. Daley that September would have required national retail chains such as Wal-Mart and Target to pay their Chicago employees at least $9.25 an hour plus $1.50 in benefits, to increase to $10.00 an hour and $3.00 in benefits by the year 2010. The law would have applied only to retail stores with at least 90,000 indoor square feet, owned by national companies with annual revenues of $1 billion or more.

If Mayor Daley had not vetoed this ordinance, it's likely the law would have ended up in court, where it would probably have been rejected, as a similar law in Maryland was. Advocates of the ordinance, both black and white, claimed it would help poor black Americans. But support for this ordinance did not begin in the black community, nor would its effect be to benefit blacks.

This scheme started as a labor union initiative introduced in cities around the country with backing by ACORN (Association of Community Organizations for Reform Now), a highly partisan left-wing advocacy group based in Washington, D.C. ACORN runs voter registration drives that benefit Democrats, while claiming it's a nonpartisan organization. Its aggressive tactics recently prompted the U.S. House of Representatives to take action.

The idea of the bill was to increase labor union membership and dues collection and put union leaders in a stronger position in dealing with the management of Wal-Mart and other nonunion companies. When two groups collaborate - in this case, unions and the black community - where the stakes are not equal, one usually reaps all the benefits while the other foots the bill. In this case, an underdeveloped black community stood to lose jobs and services.

The law would have raised the minimum wage for large, nonunion stores, forcing them to pay as much as or more than their smaller, unionized competitors. Businesses pay lower wages to people whose lack of skills and experience mean they don't add a lot of value to the goods and services the businesses sell. Many such people are young, attended low-quality public schools and may have dropped out of them, or are ex-offenders trying to get back into the workforce. A disproportionate number of these people, regrettably, are black.

So when a city government steps in and makes it illegal for some businesses to pay less than $10.00 an hour and an additional $3.00 an hour in benefits, it effectively makes it illegal for those businesses to hire many black applicants. Crucial entry-level jobs that would enable young blacks and ex-offenders to start climbing the career ladder to better-paying and more fulfilling jobs would be closed to them.

When the city council passed this ordinance, Wal-Mart indicated that it would build more stores outside of Chicago or just across the city line, and still serve Chicago citizens. Target announced it might cancel plans to build new stores in the city. The loss to the black community would have been plain to see if the mayor had not used his veto pen for the first time in seventeen years. This ordinance was not about helping the black community, but instead all about benefiting union leaders in Chicago, who are trying to protect their current members at the expense of the black community.

Although everyone wants to earn the highest wage possible, the reality of a free market system is that people are paid what they are worth to the company. This doesn't mean that an employee's value remains static. Indeed, one of the advantages of working in a place like Wal-Mart is that employees gain important job skills, management skills, and work experience that can be parlayed into future employment. Eventually, employees with significant experience should be able to start small businesses that help meet the needs of their community. Driving out stores such as Wal-Mart for paying lower wages than some people might hope for may be emotionally satisfying, but it does not help the long-term prospects of the community. Blacks will be better served by thinking about long-term goals instead of focusing on immediate rewards such as marginally higher wages.

Property Rights Benefit All

Although blacks frequently view property rights disputes as primarily affecting the rich, the Supreme Court decision in *Kelo v. City of New London* should concern us greatly. *Kelo,* the 2005 U.S. Supreme Court ruling on a case involving the economically deprived city of New London, Connecticut, should also be a wake-up call to politicians representing low-income communities and property owners regardless of neighborhood.

The real issue is eminent domain and the term "public use," which the court gave a new definition. The decision gives state and local governments permission to use eminent domain to condemn private property and turn it over to other private businesses in the name of promoting economic rejuvenation in distressed areas of the city.

What this means to low- and middle-income minority communities is that private homes connected to a distressed area can be devalued and taken if a developer wants additional land to enlarge an area of economic rejuvenation, and these properties can be turned over to developers for private use rather than public use. The U.S. Constitution plainly allows local governments to take control of private property for "public use" after payment of just compensation. But what happens if the homeowners refuse to sell their property, as happened in New London?

First of all, private property is good for individuals and for society as a whole, and government should preserve it but not interfere in its distribution. The 5-4 decision by the Supreme Court in favor of the city of New London is controversial because private property was redistributed and not all of the property seized will be given over to any actual "public use." This ignited a new debate over the term "public use" and whether private economic development can constitute a public use of property because its developers claim that they will enhance the city's tax base and create jobs to reduce high unemployment.

The *Kelo* decision was the result of decades of economic decline in New London. The end result was that the state of Connecticut deemed New London a "distressed" city, which prompted state and local officials to target it, and particularly the waterfront community of Fort Trumbull, for economic revitalization. Justice John Paul Stevens, one of the liberal justices of the court, wrote that the city was "projecting to create in excess of 1,000 jobs, an increase in taxes and would revitalize an economically distressed city, including its downtown and waterfront."

In her dissent, Justice Sandra Day O'Connor, joined by Justices Clarence Thomas, Antonin Scalia, and Chief Justice William Rehnquist, wrote, "The beneficiaries [of this decision] are likely to be those citizens with disproportionate influence and power in the political process, including large corporations and development firms." O'Connor's statement alone should have led the Congressional Black Caucus to strongly oppose the decision, as it allows any city to collude with corporate interest to deprive people of their property. Obviously our least powerful citizens will be most likely to be subjected to this form of "revitalization," and this means that blacks will be disproportionately harmed by the Court's decision.

In a separate dissent, Thomas noted that the decision would likely result in "new urban renewal projects that have historically displaced minorities, the elderly and the poor." This is a case where liberal judges are harming the economic future of African Americans with a wrongheaded decision that benefits powerful, politically connected people and harms those who are struggling to make ends meet. Private property is the key to economic security, and blacks must defend their rights to own property even - or especially - when it conflicts with grand urban renewal schemes.

Booker T. Washington encouraged blacks to focus on economic advancement over a hundred years ago. Our important struggle for equality under law sidetracked us from that goal during the past century, but it is now time for black Americans to achieve the economic independence Washington correctly advocated. America remains the land of opportunity for those willing to work hard, take risks, and adapt to the changing economy. Giving government more opportunities to override people's property rights undermines the individual initiative that makes the economy grow and allows people to struggle up out of humble circumstances. Black Americans should be especially sensitive to such efforts.

Chapter 5

Self Reliance -
Leaving Victimhood Behind

In his 1967 book, *The Crisis of the Negro Intellectual*, Harold Cruse contended that the American left of the 1950s did more harm than good to the politics and the culture of black America. The left helped create a culture of dependence, entitlement, and victimization amongst a formerly resilient people who had taken immense steps forward during the preceding decades. Unfortunately, the ideologies of the American left are still alive among many groups of blacks today. How else can you explain the recent happenings in New Orleans? In the fall of 2005, America witnessed one of the largest and longest "race card" situations in history, played out alongside a national disaster in New Orleans. Overnight, Hurricane Katrina became a national household word describing death, poverty, displacement of people, and destruction of property.

Roughly two weeks after Hurricane Katrina made landfall on the Gulf Coast, the front cover of *Newsweek* magazine showed a crying black baby, along with a headline that read, "Why Bush Failed Children of the Storm - Poverty, Race & Katrina/Lessons of a National Shame." It reminded me of the old welfare reform debate: Welfare wears a black face, even though there are more white people than black people on welfare.

I was on vacation on the East Coast when Katrina hit. I watched the news every day on every station, including cable stations and the BBC. Two images, both showing blacks only, were shown over and over and over again. One was of black children and adults looting; the other was of blacks being rescued by helicopters and boats.

One of the major daily East Coast papers ran a cartoon depicting a bus, full of people, standing on end in flood waters. The people in the back of the bus - all of whom appeared to be black - were completely under water. The water had not reached the folks in the front of the bus, who appeared to be white. At least this cartoon, exaggerated and absurd as it was, somewhat acknowledged that white people were affected by the hurricane, too. What happens to black America happens to America.

Not one black television reporter was covering the news on the air from New Orleans. Someone (I believe it was Lester Holt of NBC) had the courage to mention this on air, indicating that the wrong perception was being developed. As the media continued to play its "blacks as victims" race card, other opportunists played the political race card. Dr. Stephen J. Thurston, president of the National Baptist Convention - with an estimated 3.5 million members, one of the largest black religious groups in the country - commented, "there was a lack of response and sensitivity from the government following the Gulf Coast disaster." When Thurston blamed "the government," I don't think he was including the black Democratic mayor of New Orleans or the Democratic governor of Louisiana. He was blaming the Republican, President Bush.

On September 7, at the National Baptist Convention's annual meeting in Miami, Howard Dean, national chairman of the Democratic Party, told his audience that race was a factor in the death toll from Hurricane Katrina. He said, "We must come to terms with the ugly truth that skin color, age, and economics played a deadly role in who survived and who did not."

The strategy of whipping blacks up into a frenzy every time we discover we live in an imperfect society does nothing except replace our creative energy with negative energy. Only we can choose to steer clear of this tactic and move on to more constructive, creative, workable strategies. The only antidotes I know of that will begin to address racism in America are education and economics. That's where we should be focusing our efforts.

Holding people responsible for their actions is the key, and sometimes it can take a crisis before our leaders come to this realization. New Orleans Mayor Ray Nagin, speaking in a press interview after the hurricane, used the term "Chocolate City" to describe his vision for New Orleans. That caused some controversy among non-blacks, who thought it was a poor choice of words in a situation where you are trying to rebuild and reunite a devastated city. He later apologized for his remarks, but he reaffirmed that New Orleans would continue to be a majority African-American city.

Mayor Nagin won a tight re-election campaign in 2006. He has received billions of federal dollars to help rebuild the city and prepare for future hurricanes. Most of his displaced citizens have yet to return. According to the 2000 census, New Orleans had 484,674 residents. Today, estimates are between 192,000 and 220,000.

Although the city's population had been reduced by half, it experienced a significant crime wave following Katrina. The mayor had not expected this. When I read about the crime wave, in an Associated Press story on June 20, 2006 "National Guard ordered to New Orleans," I wondered: When are we as a community going to rise up in righteous indignation and put a stop to this? When will we step forward to halt the damage inflicted by a small group of rogues who become a cancer within our communities?

Mayor Nagin eloquently answered my question in the following words: "Today is a day when New Orleanians are stepping up," the mayor said. "We've had enough. This is our line in the sand. We're saying we're not going any further." The mayor had personally asked Gov. Kathleen Blanco to send as many as three hundred National Guardsmen and sixty state police officers to help restore order in his city after five teenagers in an SUV were shot and killed in the city's deadliest attack in eleven years.

My question - when will we rise up and put a stop to this? - is important not only for New Orleans. There are many cities, including Chicago, where the question must be answered. It's wake-up time. I hope there is someone in black Chicago and other American cities who will show the courage of Mayor Ray Nagin in confronting the high crime rates in black neighborhoods. Blacks can no longer allow criminals to control their neighborhoods and perpetuate the popular conception of blacks as violent and antisocial. A small minority of hooligans must not be allowed to hold our communities hostage anymore.

Cosby's Critique of Liberalism

The Katrina fiasco was foreshadowed in a way by the controversy kicked up by Bill Cosby the previous year. The comedian and television star brought upon himself a firestorm of criticism when he dared to question liberal assumptions about the way to success. In July 2004, Cosby celebrated his 67th birthday. Among other achievements, he had created one of the most popular TV sitcoms of all times, The Cosby Show. And in just minutes of a speech before a crowd in black tie, Cosby created a controversial - and hugely important - national discussion on black Americans and family values.

On May 17 of that year, the NAACP celebrated the 50th anniversary of *Brown v. Board of Education* at Constitution Hall in Washington, D.C. Several hundred people heard a brief address by Cosby. I doubt that the

Washington Post and Associated Press knew their reporting of Cosby's remarks the next day would turn into a national story that would run for the next two months. Two weeks into July, *The New York Times* was still covering the story, publishing a series of letters displaying mixed reactions to the conversation Cosby started by providing some old-fashioned common sense about the lack of community values and poor acceptance of personal responsibility within the black community, and among black youth in particular.

> The lower economic people are not holding up their end in this deal. These people are not parenting. They are buying things for their kids: $500 sneakers for what? And won't spend $200 for "Hooked on Phonics." I can't even talk the way these people talk: "Why you ain't?" "Where you is?" And I blamed the kid until I heard the mother talk and I heard the father talk. Everybody knows it's important to speak English - except these knuckleheads. You can't be a doctor with that kind of crap coming out of your mouth!

After listening to and reading about the national "Cosby conversation," Jamal Watson, a journalism professor and summer fellow at the *Chicago Tribune*, hit the nail right on the head in the July 18 issue of that year: "We fear that our failure to defend African-Americans at all cost will force some to call into question the authenticity of our blackness."

Some of Cosby's detractors, Watson said, "wanted to convince white folks that Cosby had gotten it all wrong - that the drug dealing, the gangs, and the school dropout rate of these wayward inner-city black youth weren't as bad as America's favorite television dad made them appear. Privately, of course, they had been talking about the problems of 'these people' for years." Debra Dickerson's 2005 book, *The End of Blackness*, described such mixed reactions from a few civil rights leaders and others when she wrote, "[blacks] have yet to realize that black autonomy is not whites' to bestow - it is blacks' to exercise."[28]

Two years before Cosby's comments at the *Brown v. Board of Education* celebration made headlines, he delivered a commencement address at Howard University. His remarks were titled "Are You Dead?" by which I understood him to mean, "If you are alive, why aren't you

---

[28] Debra Dickerson, *The End of Blackness*, (Pantheon, 2005)

achieving more?" Those remarks drew little or no attention. I also watched a television panel discussion about Cosby's comments where Cosby was one of the panelists. Only one panelist completely disagreed with Cosby; and he contributed the typical rhetorical denial: "You should not blame [us] blacks, blame the white man," he said.

I can still remember, when I was a youngster, my mother's concern about my "proper behavior" when we went downtown. She would say to me, "Boy, don't you embarrass me in front of white folks" (as if my behavior was important to them). Today, as Cosby pointed out, many children have gone well beyond merely "embarrassing" their parents. For too many of them, their conduct is sending them right to jail uneducated - or worse, to an early grave. Yet much of our liberal leadership is in denial. It observes such behavior without comment - until the "white folks" hear someone talk about what they already know all too well.

The paradox is stunning. A black man, Bill Cosby, is wealthy enough to give millions of dollars to black colleges. In 2003, the country had a black Secretary of State and black female National Security Advisor at the same time. The Williams sisters broke records in tennis, and Tiger Wood has set records in the game of golf that will last a generation or longer. And yet despite all of these success stories, black leaders, and by extension the black community, are still more concerned about what white folks think than about what we are actually doing. Aren't we free at last? We should be thankful for Cosby's honesty because he has stimulated thought and discussion on how the black community should address the important social, educational, and economic issues we face.

Celebrity Bill Cosby, one of the last people you'd describe as resembling Booker T. Washington, became the Booker T. we needed. He was willing to speak out and stand up for his convictions and his community, even when it meant saying things some people simply didn't want to hear. We can only hope that more men and women of courage will stand with Cosby and call the black community to leave victimization and self-destructiveness behind.

Who Speaks for Black America?

One of the main reasons for the severe outcry among blacks over what Cosby said is that in those few moments on stage, Cosby violated a key unwritten rule in the black community: You don't air your dirty linen in front of white folks. The truth of what you're saying doesn't matter to those who want to enforce the rule. You simply cannot be viewed as "blaming the victim" or "taking society off the hook." In the aftermath of Cosby's remarks, an age-old question was asked again: Who speaks for black America, and for poor blacks in particular? This question has been asked almost as many times as the sun has risen and set, since the end of slavery, yet it continues to stir debate and increase tensions among middle- and upper-income blacks.

Thanks to Bill Cosby, blacks and whites across the country have been taking sides again for the past three years. Cosby has managed to rekindle a century-old discussion with new passion. Michael Eric Dyson, professor of humanities at the University of Pennsylvania, opposes the Cosby style of "speak-out" on certain issues concerning the black community. Dyson said in an op-ed published by the *Chicago Tribune* on August 29, 2006, "I've been embroiled in a public debate with Bill Cosby about poor blacks for more than a year" because "Cosby has been harshly critical of the poor, blaming them for their plight and arguing that personal responsibility is the key to their success." Dyson has even written a book titled, *Is Bill Cosby Right? (Or Has the Black Middle Class Lost its Mind?)*.

But Dyson's book hardly settled the debate. It was followed by Tavis Smiley's *Covenant with Black America*, in late 2006, in which Smiley teamed up with Haki Madhubuti of Third World Press to publish what has been said to be the first nonfiction book by a black-owned publisher to become number one on the *New York Times* best-seller list. Many thought Smiley's book had all the right answers for the black condition. Smiley gathered a wide range of scholars who produced papers on ten different subject areas, from education to housing to economic development. The book offered myriad solutions for problems plaguing the black community and challenged the black community to take action. Although it ignored the conservative viewpoint, it was at least a call for the black community to take responsibility for its own condition.

Then there was a third book, by noted author Juan Williams, who basically said, "Cosby was just plain right." The book is well-written, as his award-winning books usually are, and his title says it all: *Enough: The Phony Leaders, Dead-End Movements, and Culture of Failure that are Undermining Black America - and What We Can Do About It*. In his book, Williams condemns the modern civil rights leaders for continuing to fight 1960s era battles in the twenty-first century. He urges blacks to reclaim the fierce spirit of self-determination that enabled blacks to rise up from slavery in post Civil-War period and stop looking to whites to solve all black problems. Williams thinks true leadership is desperately needed as today's black community struggles to combat drug addiction, broken families, crime and other social pathologies. He points out that Cosby did not criticize poor blacks; Cosby criticized black leaders who are shirking their duty to lead blacks out of self-destructive lifestyles and thought patterns.

Although the debate continues in the black community over whether or not Cosby was correct, he has contributed a needed new voice to the conversation. Surely everyone can agree that personal responsibility in the black community must play some role in dealing with issues such as crime, drugs, education, and business development.

Blacks Reflect America's Moral Decline

The cultural problems plaguing the black community have not developed in a vacuum. In many ways, our troubles are a reflection of the broader culture's moral decay. Although blacks must take responsibility for their actions and for the moral state of our communities, we cannot overlook the breakdown of traditional morality in white America either. It is another hurdle we must overcome.

The lack of ethics and respect for others that is manifested in much of contemporary black culture is really a reflection of a change in American society in general. It is evident in the business world, for example. A recently released survey by the National Association of Colleges and Employers asked companies to state the ten most important factors in hiring new recruits. The survey of the association's 1,600 members showed that the ability to communicate topped the list, followed by work experience, motivation, teamwork and leadership. Number ten on the list - yes, the very last - was the job candidate's ethical standards.

During my thirty years in corporate America, ethics always ranked high as a personal quality sought by senior management. But in an era when bottom-line results alone are driving many business decisions, have we started to overlook the importance of core ethical values? We certainly can see the fallout from declining ethical standards in corporate suites. The most egregious ethical lapses are relatively rare situations such as theft or embezzlement, but there are many other serious issues. Just look at the number of multimillion-dollar accounting scandals we have seen in large, high-profile companies. While most CEOs have made technology and re-engineering high priorities, ignoring ethics and morality in the marketplace will point corporations toward economic decline in the long run. The decline is based on a newly accepted paradigm of doing whatever it takes, regardless of ethics, to bolster the bottom line. But in that quest for higher profits and more shareholder value, we must not turn away from the core values on which American industry was built.

A striking example of the fuzzy grasp many in public life have of basic ethical principles is the case of syndicated radio talk-show host Armstrong Williams. President Bush signed the No Child Left Behind legislation into law in early 2002 to help give black children the same education that whites receive. Knowing how important this legislation was for black Americans, the U.S. Department of Education hired Williams, a conservative black commentator, to explain the benefits of the policy. In return, Mr. Williams was paid $240,000.

So what was the big deal? The problem was that Mr. Williams publicly promoted No Child Left Behind without disclosing that he had been hired as a spokesman for the program. While I don't doubt that Mr. Williams supports NCLB, his support for the program certainly carried more weight before people knew that it had been paid for, which is undoubtedly why he didn't reveal it. Therefore, at the very least he should have made it clear to his listeners and readers that he was a hired spokesman for the Department of Education. Mr. Williams argued that his actions were "an honest mistake." In an interview with the *New York Times*, he said his confusion about the matter was due to "a lack of training in journalism." I haven't heard anything about him returning the large sum of money he was paid.

With both Democrats and Republicans having given their spin on the Armstrong Williams situation, it is important to examine the real issue at hand: We have a problem with character and principle in our country. Principles are virtues we attempt to live by, and they are especially important when our actions are likely to have an effect on others. Principles have nothing to do with race, political affiliation, or ideology. And since most folks know right from wrong, little more than common sense is necessary to avoid most such ethical misunderstandings.

But in an interview with CNN, Williams said, "This is a great lesson to me." He was referring to his act of "blurring his roles as an independent conservative commentator and a paid promoter." Did he not know right from wrong before this happened? Or was his characterization of the incident as a learning experience simply an easy way to evade the consequences of scandalous behavior?

Wrongdoers seem to have developed a new strategy for dealing with the media. It's based upon the notion that a quick admission and apology should make a scandal go away. But should American journalism and American society be dominated by folks who seem to do the "right thing" only once caught? A culture of dishonesty hurts the most vulnerable among us, and blacks are disproportionately harmed by these acts, as public policies are adopted for all the wrong reasons.

While there may be a difference in opinion among reporters when covering a story, the public should be able to trust what it reads in a newspaper or sees on television as at least an honest attempt to be accurate and genuine when represented under the auspices of being "news." Whether Mr. Williams is a Democrat or a Republican or black or white isn't really important to this story. What's critical is knowing that he is an American who, like so many others, seems to operate on an "I'll apologize later if I get caught" mentality.

Of course, the true tragedy in this debacle over whether Armstrong Williams should have been paid to promote No Child Left Behind is that this story has received more attention than the policy itself. Education is the most important civil rights issue for black Americans today because our kids are getting such a poor education compared to the rest of society. That is a real scandal, and one that demands much more than an apology.

The Power of Culture

I mentioned in a previous chapter the ridiculous notion of teaching Ebonics to black students in the classroom. The Ebonics debate, however, was only a sidebar conversation to the larger dialogue revolving around the issue of language in the black community.

As some blacks take a part in authentically black discussions, have you ever heard the words "ax" for "ask" or "acrost" for "across"? I remember being told that an "ax" will cut you and "ask" will not, and "Boy, where did you hear that, out in the streets?" Well, decades later Thomas Sowell gave the answer to where blacks first heard the words "ax" and "acrost," and many other expressions, which some leaders and teachers continue to describe as black English. Sowell's book, released in 2005, is titled *Black Rednecks and White Liberals*.

Sowell is an economist and conservative scholar from Harvard (magna cum laude), Columbia University, and the University of Chicago, by way of Charlotte, North Carolina. William Julius Wilson, formerly of University of Chicago and now at Harvard, praised Sowell as follows: "Sowell is a man who does not sacrifice his principles. He is one of the most provocative and influential public intellectuals in the last half century." Sowell's research shows that white liberals who consider themselves friends of blacks are cheering a segment of blacks on towards self-destruction. He challenges today's hip-hop intellectuals as well as historic interpreters of American life, such as Alexis de Tocqueville.

The book is based on thirty years of research and documented facts that forcefully challenge current assumptions about blacks and the issues of race, racism, culture, and black identity. Sowell points out that much of what passes for black identity today is a modern version of the self-defeating culture slaves inherited from poor redneck whites who came from the poor sections of Britain and settled in southern states. Sowell found, for example, that during the First World War, white soldiers from Georgia, Arkansas, Kentucky, and Mississippi scored lower on mental tests than black soldiers from Ohio, Illinois, New York, and Pennsylvania.

White liberals come into this story, Sowell observes, because since the 1960s they have been aiding and abetting a self-destructive ghetto lifestyle that is essentially a remnant of the redneck culture which handicapped Southern whites and blacks alike. After many decades the majority of both black and white Southerners did master the King's English. Those who failed to do so are largely poor and undereducated and are certainly not models for emulation.

Sowell's book thoroughly debunks the assumption that "blacks can't do college level work or score as high as whites on tests." Supporting Sowell's research is a study published in 2005 indicating that most of the black alumni of Harvard were from either the West Indies or Africa or were the children of West Indian or African immigrants. Sowell comments:

> These people are the same race as American blacks, who greatly outnumber both groups. If this disparity is not due to race, it is equally hard to explain by racism. To a racist, one black is pretty much the same as another. But, even if a racist somehow lets his racism stop at the water's edge, how could he tell which student was the son or daughter of someone born in the West Indies or in Africa, especially since their American-born offspring probably do

not even have a foreign accent? What, then, could explain such large disparities in demographic 'representation' among these three groups? Perhaps they have different patterns of behavior and different cultures and values behind their behavior.

Slavery cannot explain the difference between American blacks and West Indian blacks living in the United States, because the ancestors of both were enslaved. When race, racism, and slavery all fail the empirical test, what is left? Again Sowell's answer is culture. Current black American culture in many ways is very ineffective at reflecting and reinforcing the conservative values that have long been the backbone of black American life. In fact it often undermines those values. Elizabeth Wright, editor of *Issues and Views*, wrote as follows about the contagion of hip-hop music in 2005:

> What's to be done after a poison has been released into the bloodstream? When, back in 1996, Delores Tucker began her campaign to raise public awareness to the socially and spiritually destructive nature of "rap" music, she and the other blacks who supported her crusade were subjected to virulent verbal attacks. And when Rev. Calvin Butts, pastor of Harlem's Abyssinian Baptist Church, led a similar campaign to denounce the "spirit-killing" vulgarity at the heart of rap, he fared no better.
>
> Now, almost a decade later, the contagion, initially spawned by desolate, angry products of turbulent households, has spread more deeply into mainstream society and has evolved into an animus known as "hip-hop." Picked up, exploited, and disseminated by an amoral breed of commercializer, the poison now infects vast numbers of youth.[29]

Although hip-hop is not the only problem facing the black community, it has become a source of ethnic identity that is extremely counterproductive. Whereas blacks should be encouraged to look to the true heroes of their past and present - men and women like Booker T. Washington, Colin Powell, Martin Luther King Jr., Zora Neal Hurston and Rosa Parks - hip-hop glorifies angry, violent, self-obsessed music stars. The

---

[29] Elizabeth Wright, "The Rap Contagion," *News & Views,* The New Coalition for Economic and Social Change, December 2005.

behavior enshrined in their music and videos encourages blacks to embrace nihilistic hedonism and self-righteous anger. Wright points out that the toxic blend of vulgarity and promotion of selfishness, sensuality, and cruelty that is endemic to hip-hop music has spread through American culture as a whole:

> In "Gangsta GOP," on "Davey D's Hip Hop Daily News," a white father, identified as John Kressler, is quoted as either boasting or complaining that his "good, Christian son" has been convinced through this musical genre "to act like a little gangbanger from the inner city," has "adopted some of [the] habits, values, and mannerisms" of his favorite rapper, and "walks around the house mimicking this new African American rap style of speech.

Both black and white liberals seemed to find it difficult to condemn this cultural phenomenon, even though much of it was clearly destructive of the moral values that make for true success and happiness. As a result, the hip-hop culture became increasingly pervasive, and the protests of those who were brave enough to speak out fell on deaf ears. Wright noted, again in 2005:

> Last month in New York City, a capacity crowd over-filled an auditorium to listen to a panel of men and women discuss "the impact of misogynistic rap on black women." The event's organizers appeared to know why they were there - to candidly air their views on what they consider the corrosive impact of rap/hip-hop's toxic lyric content on both young men and women. It turned out that a large number of those who attended also came with an agenda - to defend their hip-hop "artists" and "culture."
>
> Among these defenders were a multitude of women, who claimed to be fans of the music and its graphic videos. According to *Essence* magazine, a sponsor of the event, 10 percent of hip-hop audiotape and CD purchases are made by black women, 18 to 34. Of course, it's hard to determine the accuracy of this figure in light of the *Essence* claim that only a minuscule 7 percent of these tapes and videos are purchased by black males, 18 to 24. Are we left to speculate that the balance of this bilge is being bought by youngsters like Mr. Kressler's "good, Christian son?" It is a maxim, often repeated, that the major purchasers of this pseudo-ghetto sludge are young white males.

With a population of females who enjoy the degrading lyrics and pornographic images of women as worthless, throw-away objects of pleasure, it's no surprise that the meeting, intended to "debate" the controversies surrounding rap, devolved into chaotic shouting matches. Views of the panelists were met with jeers, boos, and catcalls from the audience. One report claims that the session "ended abruptly, with little solution-oriented discourse." Delores Tucker and Rev. Butts could have told them that and saved the expense and disappointment.

The cultural decay evident in hip-hop is reflected in the appalling amount of black-on-black violence in our nation's cities. The reality of black youth killing other blacks has been cemented in our collective consciousness through Hollywood films, nightly news reports, and sociological studies. Yet as our race has attacked itself, the so-called "black leadership" has hardly raised its voice in protest. An April 29, 2003, editorial in the *Chicago Sun-Times*, "Where's the outrage over violence against our kids?" spoke volumes about the unfathomably misplaced basic priorities of the black leadership in Chicago. I know it was only a coincidence that this editorial ran on the same day Rev. Jesse Jackson's column, "Silicon Valley Can Rise Again," appeared in the *Sun-Times* and was placed next to it. But the irony was nonetheless startling. There is a wide gulf between the *Sun-Times'* editorial raising the question of the lifespan of Chicago's black youth and Jesse Jackson's concerns about Silicon Valley.

At the national level, the NAACP seems to have no better idea of how to address this problem than to sue the gun manufacturers. That's not a response that will do any real good: we don't shoot the cow because someone let the milk spoil and kids drank it anyway. In other words, the problem this time is as much in the community as it is at City Hall. How many more kids must die like hogs, to use poet Claude McKay's words, before Chicago's black leadership shows real concern and makes an effort toward genuine solutions?

The well-known fact that blacks account for a disproportionately large amount of crime in this country has not been lost on the shapers of public opinion. When these public figures mention the statistics or make reference to the tragedy of black crime, however, they often perpetuate the stereotype that blacks are naturally more prone to criminality than others, thereby adding to mistrust among the races.

As a black conservative, I was appalled by William Bennett's comments on the radio program "Morning in America," on September 28, 2005. Public figures may think whatever they want, but what they say should not be racially destructive in any way. Bennett said, "But I do know that it's true that if you wanted to reduce crime, you could, if that were your sole purpose, you could abort every black baby in the country and your crime rate would go down." He pointed out that it would be "an impossible, ridiculous, and morally reprehensible thing to do," but then repeated the main point: "but your crime rate would go down."

Bennett is strongly opposed to abortion, so what he said was meant to ridicule and distance himself from the kind of reasoning that would justify killing unborn children in order to achieve some uncertain social benefit decades later. His mistake was to validate the underlying assumption that more black children than white children are destined to become criminals. That is shameful and wrong.

High rates of black criminality have nothing to do with genetics or what takes place in the womb, and everything to do with families, schools, neighborhoods, and workplaces. A black child born to an intact family, able to attend schools that are safe and effective and play in a neighborhood that is safe and full of good role models, is unlikely grow up to become a criminal. It is just as unlikely a prospect for that black child as it would be for a white child born to similar circumstances.

While race plays a part in a many aspects of American life, we cannot continue deluding ourselves into thinking it explains everything. When kids are being killed by stray bullets, and those bullets are coming from African Americans, it's not because of the color of the shooters' skin but the content of their character. Working to improve the social conditions under which blacks grow up is an essential step in fixing the problem, and that includes both giving them access to better schools and requiring them to live up to high moral standards. One thing the public schools and hip-hop culture have in common is that they both trap black children in a culture that leads all too easily to failure and delinquency.

Although I have mentioned Rev. Jesse Jackson, I do not by any means put all the blame on him. No one elected or appointed him to be concerned about anybody's kids except his own. There are three elected congressmen - as well as state and city elected officials - in Chicago who represent the wards where drugs and killings have reached the terrorist level almost on a weekly basis. Rather than taking on these killers, our leaders continue to decry white racism. We need to fix our own problems.

Until we in the black community reject the glorification of crime and the sexual degradation of women, we will not be able to rise up and secure our share of the American Dream. We must get rid of the negative self-image that holds us back and start treating ourselves and one another with dignity. If we want whites in America to respect us, we must first respect ourselves.

Learning from South Africa

Dr. Bennett's blunder highlights the fragile state of race relations that exists even today in the United States. It is often impossible for whites and blacks to discuss their differences openly in today's racially charged environment. Our history is supposedly too painful and white atrocities too severe to allow for even-tempered dialogue, at least until full reparations have been paid, whatever those might be. If this is true, there was something strikingly absent from a 1996 visit to Chicago by South Africa's Deputy President Thabo M. Mbeki. While he was here on a clear mission to urge local companies to invest in the new South Africa, he never once suggested that U.S. companies should invest in his homeland to undo the wrongs of apartheid.

During a reception and dinner hosted by the Chicago Council on Foreign Relations, Mr. Mbeki articulated the need for job-creating economic growth in South Africa. Not once, however - either directly or indirectly - did he mention to a mostly white audience of business people how whites had treated President Nelson Mandela during his twenty-seven years in prison or Mbeki's own twenty-seven years in exile. He never suggested that the United States should invest in South Africa because we owe it to the country due to U.S.-imposed sanctions or any other injustices, such as minimal amounts of foreign aid dollars.

Instead, he made it clear that as a foreign policy it is in America's best interest to help South Africa develop its infrastructure by investing there. In spite of obvious past hardship, he always talked about the present and the future of his country as a major player on the world stage. He didn't dwell on the past.

What a stark contrast between South Africa's new black leadership as it deals with corporate America and the U.S. government, and how the black American leadership negotiates with those same parties! This difference in management style may have a direct impact on how both styles of leadership translate into public policy.

One style, I argue, has led us into excessive attitudes of victimization and dependency, while the other is leading toward self-reliance and a relationship of equals as international trading partners. As I listened to Mr. Mbeki's presentation and talked to him afterward, I discovered that his message was the same whenever he spoke. Among the others who heard the same message during the dignitaries' visit to Chicago were executives already doing business in South Africa: John H. Johnson of Johnson Publishing Co., John H. Bryan of Sara Lee Corp., and Jory Luster of Luster Products. Others will certainly follow. South Africa may be one of the last frontiers where large and small companies (and American blacks, in particular) will have the opportunity to play a major role through investments in helping a new democracy grow stronger.

I am mindful of the statement Mr. Mandela made during his inaugural speech: "As we were liberated from our own fear, our presence automatically liberates others." As the world welcomed the new South Africa in 1994, businessmen and -women forged links on every continent, and hostilities changed to handshakes. Nelson Mandela's actions reinforced an old Booker T. Washington adage: "Character is true power." And in any contest between character and power, character will win in the end.

A New Way of Thinking

It's time for new thinking and a new beginning in American race relations. Scripturally, it's called "the renewing of your mind." Our black communities are falling apart, and our morals, values, and ethics are being dismantled. New thinking means "no more excuses" and focusing on the end result. James Forten (1766-1842), the famous black businessman and inventor, spent a lifetime reminding blacks that America was "the land that gave us birth, and which many of us fought for, during the war which established our Independence."[30] And, he notes, "whether they cared to admit it or not, black men had helped to found the nation."

Yet more than a few viewed Bill Cosby's straight talk, noted earlier, as

---

[30] Julie Winch, "James Forten, Conservative Radical," in *Black Conservatism: Essays in Intellectual and Political History,* edited by Peter Eisenstadt (New York, NY: Garland, 1999).

being negative and an instance of blaming the victim. The lesson I took from Cosby was best expressed by Booker T. Washington over a hundred years ago: "No one should seek to close his eyes to the truth that the race is passing through a very serious and trying period of its development, a period that calls for the use of our ripest thought." The point that Washington was making then, and is as true as ever now, is that we must reverse the negative thinking that allows us to excuse failure. Rather than simply making resolutions to reverse the negatives, we should instead assess our strengths to generate new thoughts and create a new beginning. Each of us can make a difference in our own way. For example, we can:

- resolve to involve ourselves in our child(ren)'s school in a positive way;
- spend more time with our children, taking them to cultural events, or even just reading books together;
- monitor our children's TV watching, music, and reading material; and
- take classes for self-improvement.

Any of these things can help make today better than yesterday. And each is a demonstration that black Americans are collectively embracing a new way of thinking that will liberate us for real success.

Chapter 6

Politics - Democrats, Republicans, and Blacks

Our democratic system in the past and for the foreseeable future will be based on a two-party system: Democrats and Republicans. Yet some segments of the black community - America's largest and one of its oldest ethnic or racial groups - have been unable to accept the fact that there is an alternative to the Democratic Party. The result is that blacks have been taken for granted by the Democratic Party for more than fifty years.

We must remember that the political strength of ethnic groups in America has depended upon their ability to leverage the political system so that politicians do not take them for granted. To accomplish that, ethnic groups cannot be so inflexible that a rival party views them as impossible to woo. For black Americans to continue voting almost as a one-party state in a two-party system negates the true essence of the 1965 Voting Rights Act. It's ineffective politically for blacks to continue to allow themselves to be taken for granted by the Democrats and largely dismissed as unwinnable by the Republicans. It doesn't serve the people, nor does it benefit the two-party system. In addition, our youth are growing up experiencing segregated voting patterns. They don't even know what a split ticket is.

While the two-party system is not perfect, it continues to be the best in the world. And as history has shown us that the two-party system can work for other minorities, it can work more effectively for blacks. My argument is not that it's wrong for nearly 90 percent of blacks to vote for one party, but that we are not part of the competition for both parties. Voting was the dream and the struggle. Why not use it wisely?

The black community should follow the lead of the Latino community and learn to flex its political muscles. To do so, blacks must make it clear that they will no longer automatically vote Democratic. Nationally, both major parties are watching the growth of the Latino population quite closely and are giving serious attention to their needs in an effort to court their vote.

A poll commissioned by United Neighborhood Organization (UNO), one of Chicago's largest Hispanic community-based organizations, shows that the usual media view of Hispanics being a disadvantaged group - one that is being victimized by discrimination and dependent on civil rights or affirmative action laws and entitlements - is not accurate.[31] The research shows that the Hispanics here seek to embrace opportunity and the American dream and strongly believe they can achieve it. UNO President Juan Rangel would like to drop the label "minority," as it doesn't foster a positive perception of those seeking to become part of the American mainstream, which is the goal of Chicago-area Hispanics, according to UNO's poll.

Other groups that have discovered how to win political gains include Asian Americans and Indians. A 2005 article by Sara Kugler for the Associated Press described how New York's Democrat and Republican candidates for mayor wooed the Asian vote. I was struck most by how Asians account for only 11 percent of NYC's population while blacks are 26 percent and Hispanics are 28 percent. How did such a small group get the attention of the city's political leaders?

I think there are two reasons. First, Asians are leapfrogging blacks because the former want to be mainstream Americans. Too few blacks do, and those who have achieved it are often afraid to speak out. I know black executives and middle-managers who stay silent and on the sidelines, allowing an aging generation of professional race activists to present themselves as role models and spokespersons for the black community. Their messages focus on victimhood and entitlement instead of self-help and virtuous behavior.

Second, as Kugler writes, "the city's Asian voters appear to be up for grabs. Exit polls find that while the majority of Asian voters in New York City are registered Democrats, they are willing to cross party lines for the right candidates." The same cannot be said of blacks, who seem willing to vote Democrat no matter how corrupt, incompetent, or dishonest the candidates in that party.

Poll after poll and survey after survey has confirmed how strong and persistent partisanship voting among black Americans has been over the

---

[31] Juan Rangel, Minority Assumptions, Hispanic Realities: Voices of Optimism," *Survey Findings January, 2003,* United Neighborhood Organization, 2003.

past few decades, to the great benefit of the Democratic Party. Despite the high proportion of black votes going to Democrats, who are on the whole much more liberal than their Republican opponents, relatively few blacks identify themselves as "liberals." As previously mentioned, 33 percent of blacks characterized themselves as conservative, 30 percent as moderate, and only 29 percent as liberal in 1992, a period of liberal dominance.

Blacks are liberal on some issues and conservative on others, and therefore there should be much more constructive debate and free thinking on the issues. We should want to know how much support there is from conservative blacks for ideas that can improve our current civil rights agenda and expand the economy, fix our public education system, prepare young people and adults for better jobs, and combat drugs and crime.

Black America Must Speak with Many Voices, Not One

Part of the problem in the black community is the view that there can only be one or two authentic black leaders at any given time. Although there are always aspiring leaders fighting to be heard, we keep coming back to one key question: Who speaks for blacks? A few years ago *Newsweek* ran a cover story asking the question, "Black like Who?" Since the death of the Rev. Martin Luther King Jr., this question has come up frequently. Behind the question always lies another one: Has this leader been sanctioned by the proper group of blacks? For the past thirty years, the sanctioning of leadership has been in the hands of a few civil rights organizations and established political leaders.

But what happens to those blacks who are not chosen by the traditional leadership or who challenge their vision on race? Or what if their political views are not the same as those of the traditional leadership? Is there room for compromise, or must black leaders deemed politically incorrect by the black establishment invariably be anathematized and silenced?

A vivid example of black organizations' ongoing process of eliminating dissenting voices was when the Rev. Jimmie Daniels, National President of Operation Push, was asked to resign simply because he'd had a meeting with House Speaker Newt Gingrich, a Republican. What makes this even more ludicrous is that the Rev. Jesse Jackson would later invite Mr. Gingrich on his TV show, although he was and continued to be highly critical of the congressman's stand on welfare reform. Rep. Gingrich then invited Rev. Jackson to be his guest when President Clinton delivered his

State of the Union address, yet the Rev. Jackson experienced no negative press as a result. The contradictions abound.

Similarly, when many people were trying to draft retired Gen. Colin Powell to run for president in 1996, there was a select group of community and political leaders saying that Gen. Powell was not "black enough," whatever that could possibly mean. The example that hit me closest to home was when I was confirmed by the Illinois Senate for the position of trustee of the Illinois Board of Community Colleges in 1996. My nomination was dogged by controversy. The big question among African-American legislators was whether I (a Republican) was "the right kind" of black.

I think we have moved beyond the era of having a single leader with a single view of who speaks for blacks. It's time for self-responsibility and new voices as we move into the twenty-first century.

Blacks, Republicans, and Ronald Reagan

The complete estrangement of blacks from the Republican Party was clearly revealed in 2004 when President Reagan died. Many blacks in leadership positions were either silent during the week of mourning for the death of the President, or bitter in their persistent criticism of the man. A commentary posted on BET.com said, "Reagan began a sustained attack on the government's civil rights apparatus, opened an assault on affirmative action and social welfare programs, [and] embraced the white racist leaders of then-apartheid South Africa."

What I saw and experienced was very different, and for that opportunity I thank two friends, Gloria Toote and Henry Lucas. Both were very close to President Reagan. I campaigned for Reagan in 1980, and in 1984 I served as State Chairman of Illinois Black Republicans for Reagan/Bush. That year, I and five other conservative blacks placed, at our own expense, a full-page ad in *Jet magazine* presenting Reagan's very commendable record on civil rights and economic opportunity for blacks. The President received 10 percent of the black vote. I was fortunate enough to make many visits to the White House. The Reagan I met was comfortable around blacks, aware of the difficulties we faced, and committed to building a more inclusive Republican Party and leveling the playing field.

Criticism of Reagan from black spokespersons is motivated by ideology, not an objective review of policies adopted during Reagan's eight years in office or the status of black Americans. Reagan increased funding for civil rights enforcement, and his Justice Department brought more suits to enforce voting rights in its first three years than the Carter administration had in four years. And of course, Reagan signed legislation making Martin Luther King Day a national holiday.

Blacks did well under Reagan, too. The black middle class started its strong drive upward during the Reagan years, as reliance on government became less of an option, and economic growth and prosperity helped everyone's boat rise. The Reagan tax cuts were a boon for black businesses and entrepreneurs no less than for whites, and millions of black Americans went to college, became homeowners, and started achieving the American Dream as a result of the expanding economy that was a direct product of those tax cuts and removal of countless unnecessary government strictures on business..

The leaders of most black advocacy groups still refuse to see this, much less admit it. They are still liberal advocates of bigger government, and so they blame Reagan for their loss of political power and relevancy. Reagan was sincerely committed to ending racial discrimination and helping blacks advance socially and economically. It wasn't a show. On November 26, 1984, the President wrote to me, "Unfortunately, my crusade against bigotry and prejudice isn't often heard above the political rhetoric. I appreciate all your help."

My friend Henry Lucas, the first black member of the Republican National Committee, recalled that President Reagan, immediately before his inauguration, asked him (in Henry's words) "how to proceed in bringing about equality for African Americans." Henry replied, "we must do everything we can to level the playing field." Several years later, Reagan still remembered the conversation. After saving Meharry Medical College in Nashville, Tennessee, by approving a $50 million grant, Reagan asked Henry, "Are we leveling the playing field?" Henry replied, "Yes, Mr. President, we are beginning to level the playing field."

The Media, Politics, and Blacks

President Reagan wasn't the only Republican or conservative to get the cold shoulder from the self-proclaimed black leadership. Blacks who happen to be Republicans or conservatives are smeared and slandered just as badly today as Clarence Thomas was during his confirmation hearings in 1991. One recent example is the controversy surrounding Judge Janice Rogers

Brown, the first black female to sit on the California Supreme Court.

Judge Brown was nominated in 2003 to the U.S. Court of Appeals for the District of Columbia, but she was not confirmed until 2005. Civil rights organizations and the Congressional Black Caucus argued that Judge Brown was basically unfit to serve on the D.C. Court, a traditional stepping stone to the U.S. Supreme Court. To make their point, they described her as "to the right of Supreme Court Justice Antonin Scalia and Justice Clarence Thomas." That was supposed to be the hammer and nail through the heart, ensuring her nomination would be dead on arrival in the up-or-down vote in the full Senate. It was a strong statement of disapproval from leading black organizations about this particular black female.

It also condemns those groups as either disingenuous or irresponsible or both. Where were the state NAACP and the Los Angeles NAACP for the previous ten years if Judge Brown was as bad for black folks as they were saying while her confirmation was pending? Where were the black politicians in California when she needed people to defend her obvious qualifications? True, she was appointed by a Republican governor, but she was re-elected with 76 percent of the state's votes, the highest vote percentage of all justices on the ballot. Yet there was little public support for her from blacks. A bipartisan group of sixteen California law professors praised Judge Brown. The *San Francisco Chronicle* supported her in an editorial. As a single mother who worked her way through college and law school, she should be a role model to many.

Further scrutiny of some of the same records reveals something quite different from what was reported in the media. The following excerpt is from a letter dated October 21, 2003, on stationery that read Court of Appeals State of California, 300 South St., Los Angeles, Ca., addressed to Sen. Orrin G. Hatch (R-Utah) with a copy to Sen. Patrick J. Leahy (D-Vermont): "This letter is written in support of Janice Rogers Brown as a Judge of the US Court of Appeals. In her role as a Justice of the California Supreme Court, Justice Brown has served California well." Such a letter should carry as much or more weight as the study by the left-wing advocacy group People for the American Way, which the NAACP used to slander Judge Brown.

For a long time, Supreme Court Justice Clarence Thomas was the prime target for this type of attack. Even today, some charge him with not being authentically black. Audiences encourage this sort of behavior. If a speaker's opening remarks include some inappropriate joke or nasty wisecrack about Justice Thomas, everybody laughs. The ice is broken, the speaker has the audience in the palm of his hand, and everything he says afterwards is taken as gospel.

More recently, Colin Powell and Condoleezza Rice have taken their turns as the critics' targets, and Justice Thomas has gotten something of a reprieve. So here you have three of the most successful black persons of our time, known and admired the world over, ... and most popular black journalists and academics criticize them mercilessly. We should be pointing to them as examples to follow. We should be pointing to them as role models, not poster people for what happens to those who dare to convey any kind of alternative to a leftist, statist political agenda!

As I have observed this attack-mode trend, I thought at first it was just a matter of intense opposition to black Republicans, which one could understand as simple nasty partisanship, while not excusing it. But then came Bill Cosby, a non-Republican, and the same furious attacks were pointed in his direction. We often make a point of chastising the non-black world, reminding them that "All blacks don't look alike" and "all blacks don't think alike." And of course that's true. But within our own community, we refuse to accept even slightly divergent views. That is a recipe for political and social disaster, and following generations continue to pay the price for the black leadership's monolithic devotion to a leftist, statist political agenda.

Out-of-Step NAACP Must Reclaim its Vision

The organization that bears the most responsibility for the sorry state of black leadership is the NAACP. The National Association for the Advancement of Colored People (NAACP) held its 90th annual convention in September 1999 in New York City, the organization's birthplace at the beginning of the twentieth century. The biggest accomplishments of the convention: assailing major TV networks for not having a single black person in a major role in any of the twenty six new shows for the new season and the movie industry for not hiring enough blacks, along with a move to sue gun manufacturers. Of course there was also a call to the organization's 2,000-plus chapters around the country to produce the largest voter registration drive in history in order to elect a Democrat as president.

What the convention showed most vividly was how weak and confused the NAACP was as it entered its 91st year and a new century. The

NAACP's priorities, as indicated by the outcome of its convention, have nothing to do with the current obstacles faced by most blacks. In fact, the networks' potential alienation of black teenagers from television might be a blessing in disguise, given that black students are spending nearly three times as many hours watching television as they do studying.

The NAACP convention did little to address the issues that have a direct impact on black America: ruptured families, high crime rates, a public school system that is failing its students worse than ever, teen pregnancies, increasing numbers of young black males going to prison, and African-Americans falling way behind in computer literacy. Just a few months before the dawn of the new millennium, the NAACP missed a clear opportunity to have a strategic discussion of the future of the civil rights movement in the next century and open it to new ideas that can replace the failed policies of recent years.

That discussion is sorely needed. A *Detroit News* survey in 1992 revealed that 94 percent of black Americans thought the NAACP was out of touch with the everyday problems of most blacks - the poor in particular.[32] After the leadership problems in subsequent years - problems that never resulted in needed organizational changes - it's questionable that the NAACP is any more in touch today than it was then.

The 1992 resignation of Benjamin Hooks provided the NAACP with a missed opportunity to downsize personnel, restructure its ineffective and oversized national board, and rethink its mission in light of issues facing African-Americans today. Instead, the organization's board of directors, and Chairman William F. Gibson in particular, refused to acknowledge that the organization was in the throes of a leadership crisis. A signal that something was very wrong was the political ouster and/or resignation of a number of important figures, including Percy Sutton, a businessman and former Manhattan borough president.

Yet Mr. Gibson moved ahead, and with the support of the board he selected Benjamin Chavis to turn around an organization that was out of touch with its constituency and faced with serious financial, managerial, and membership problems. Seventeen months later and after much embarrassment, Chavis was fired - the first top-level firing in the organization's eighty-five-year history. Chavis' professional experience was

---

[32] Detroit News Survey quoted by Rhonda Chriss Lokeman, "The good fight," in *The Kansas Star*, February 2, 1992.

a mismatch for the crisis the organization was in. He should have never been selected in the first place. Chavis' popularity stemmed from his nearly 10 year imprisonment after being convicted of conspiracy and arson. The charges were eventually dropped and Chavis became an icon of the civil rights movement. However, with the exception of his work with Dr. King on the Southern Christian Leadership Council (SCLC), Chavis did not have enough management experience to lead a national organization.

Mr. Chavis and his supporters wanted us to believe that some Jewish and corporate leaders brought about his demise. But it's an insult to think that we should overlook allegations of mismanagement of the organization's limited resources, mishandled sexual harassment charges, and his flow of misinformation to board members.

The recent debacle surrounding the unexpected resignation of President Bruce Gordon further demonstrates the leadership vacuum in the NAACP. Mr. Gordon apparently felt micro-managed by Julian Bond, Chairman of the Board, and resented it. His resignation left the NAACP once again struggling to find a leader capable of righting the ship. The real problem is that the NAACP, as currently constituted, is increasingly irrelevant, operating with obsolete values amid significant changes in America and the world. The major issues faced during the civil rights era are for the most part over, yet the organization is still largely directed by 1960s era leaders.

Foremost among the challenges we face today, in my view, are a lack of self-reliance at a community level, high crime rates in our communities, a public school system that desperately needs restructuring, the huge number of teen pregnancies, and too many young males in prison. Until and unless the NAACP redirects its mission to tackle these challenges, it will not recover from its current crisis. The NAACP must lead on the basis of these priorities, or the organization will be remain ineffective and become completely irrelevant. The NAACP cannot sustain itself if it limits itself to whistle blowing and rooting out racism from the public sphere when the real accomplishments today are being made through education and entrepreneurship.

Chapter 7

Modern Conservative Blacks

Writer George Schuyler (1895-1977) described what it meant to be a conservative black in his 1965 autobiography, *Black and Conservative.* Schuyler, a columnist for the *Pittsburgh Courier* and a contributor to the conservative *National Review,* wrote in his autobiography that the black American is "not given to gambling what advantages he has in quixotic adventures. The ability to conserve, consolidate and change when expedient, is the hallmark of individual and group intelligence... The Negro had adjusted to every change with the basic aim of survival and advancement."[33]

Although many people do not think of Martin Luther King as a conservative, he championed many of the same principles as today's black conservatives. He argued for quality education, personal integrity, public morality, equal treatment under the law, and a color-blind society. I believe that Dr. King must be included in any discussion of black individuals who carried the conservative banner. Other black heroes who have been claimed by the left also merit consideration for their conservative views. The following is a personal reflection on my experiences with Dr. King and other black leaders who acted on conservative principles.

Dr. King was born in Atlanta, Georgia, to an influential and well-educated middle-class family. He started the Southern Christian Leadership Conference (SCLC) in Atlanta and was living in Atlanta when he was killed. Still, most folks think of Montgomery or Birmingham when his name is mentioned.

I walked past Dr. King's house twice a day on my way to and from Alabama State University for two years, a three mile walk from where I lived. Dr. King was often seen walking across the campus, perhaps to some meeting regarding the bus boycott. The first-year English professor was secretary of the bus boycott committee, which was known as the MIA

---

[33] George Schuyler, *Black and Conservative* (New Rochelle, NY: Arlington House, 1966).

91

(Montgomery Improvement Association).

The boycott started in December 1955 and ended 382 days later. I played no leadership role in the boycott. I was just a follower who went to meetings to know what was happening. The committee once needed a group of boys to stand in shifts guarding Dr. King's house. Since assuming leadership of the movement in Montgomery, his house had been bombed by violent white supremacists and the town was afraid the extremists would return. I eagerly signed up for the task of guarding the house. The boycott was not a difficult time for me personally. Most of us didn't have cars, and during the time I spent in Troy there were no city buses at all. So walking instead of riding where you wanted to go presented no problem to most of us students, both high school and college.

My first encounter with Dr. King came when I was in high school. I was living in Montgomery, Alabama, part of the time during the bus boycott of 1955. Since then, I have heard and read many different versions about how the Montgomery bus boycott started. Many of the whites in Montgomery thought the NAACP started the bus boycott in order to have a legal test case, because they knew Mrs. Parks had been the past secretary of the local chapter of the organization. Although the boycott did become a legal test case, the NAACP did not start it, and Mrs. Parks was not a "plant" as the media and the mayor's office were suggesting. A local labor leader and past president of the NAACP, however, was deeply involved in the boycott as a community activist.

I grew up living between Troy and Montgomery; a distance of thirty-eight miles. Troy was a small city, and Montgomery was much larger. Montgomery, one of the oldest cities in America, is known as "the cradle of the Confederacy." It is the city where Jefferson Davis took his oath of office as president of the Confederate States of America. It was in Montgomery that the first Confederate flag was made. It is the city that introduced the 26 year-old Rev. Dr. Martin Luther King Jr. to the nation and the world stage.

Just before the bus boycott, the racial mood among blacks in Montgomery had reached a level where people knew something had to be done regarding race relations in general, and dealing with the Montgomery bus line in particular. The big question among the leadership was who would step forth and speak out. The Emmett Till killing had just happened next door in Mississippi. It was in the national news, and it created a climate of hate and fear.

A similar situation had just happened in Montgomery, where a young black boy was accused of whistling at a white woman, put in jail, and then killed while in jail. At the trial the woman said she lied and was sorry, but the judge told her she was lying in court and had told the truth to the police. After the boy was murdered by a white mob, a jury found no one guilty for the young man's death.

Around that same time, a number of black women and students had been put off the city buses because they refused to give their seat when a white person was standing. One of the cases involved a twelve-year-old girl. The judge had promised the local black leadership that he would not put the girl in jail and give her a criminal record, but he did so anyway.

Then a college woman named Rosa Parks, who worked at the leading department store in downtown Birmingham, was taken off the bus and jailed. Mrs. Parks had seen many other black men, women, and children put off the buses to make room for white passengers. Mrs. Parks knew it was city law, but she had made up her mind if it ever happened to her she would not move. On Thursday, December 1, 1955, at about 5:00 p.m., it happened. The driver wanted a couple of seats for whites and called back for some blacks to move. Three blacks moved immediately. Mrs. Parks was asked to move. She quietly refused and was arrested by the police.

Mrs. Parks was the right person at the time, just as Jackie Robinson was the right person to integrate Major League baseball. Her character was impeccable and her dedication deep-rooted, and she was well-educated and well-respected within the black community. She had no idea what would happen next, or even whether she would be able to get bail. Even before her jailers allowed her to make a telephone call, the word had spread all over town by the people on the bus. Calls were made to the usual community leaders, but they were not home yet or in their offices.

If I may digress for a moment, I believe Rosa Parks' influence on the Civil Rights Movement extended well beyond the boycott. When she died in 2005, flags around the nation were flown at half-mast in recognition of the major contributions that Rosa Parks, in her ninety-two years of life, first in the South and then in the North, made to the history of this nation. Was it providence that 2005 also marked the fiftieth anniversary of the Montgomery bus boycott, which changed race relations across this country and introduced the world to the names Rosa Parks and Martin Luther King?

While Rosa Parks' final footprint on the civil rights movement was being the first female to lie in state in the U.S. Capitol rotunda, her greatest contribution, in my view, was bringing women to the front lines of leadership in the boycott through the Montgomery Improvement Association. Her example encouraged women throughout the country to get more involved, to lead, guide, and direct the future rather than just participate in it.

As we recognize Parks, we should also recognize that she had partners in the Montgomery struggle. One partner, often forgotten, was Jo Ann Gibson Robinson, who was an English professor at Alabama State University and the president of the Women's Political Council, the most active and assertive black civic organization in Montgomery. Robinson acted as a sort of secretary for the Montgomery Improvement Association and kept detailed records which were unknown for thirty years until they were published in 1987 under the title *The Montgomery Bus Boycott and the Women Who Started It.*

Returning to 1955, it is important to remember that when Rosa Parks took her heroic stand, she was not alone. A college professor who had been put off the bus said something had to be done, and she called several ladies who belonged to a club of which she was the president. They talked about having a one-day boycott on Monday morning. Since it was Thursday, that gave them time to plan. When the local labor leader was finally reached that night, he agreed to a one-day boycott and was able to call on a white lawyer friend of his to make bail for Mrs. Parks.

But a big question about the boycott remained: Who would step up and lead such an event? The leader's job, life, and family would be at risk. Another right person in the right place at the time, was the Rev. Dr. Martin Luther King Jr. Armed with a Ph.D. from Boston University, Dr. King had arrived in Montgomery just a year earlier in 1954, at the age of twenty-six, to serve as pastor of the influential Dexter Avenue Baptist Church. The location of Dexter Baptist made it the most prominent black church in the city, and whoever the minister was could play a unique role in the boycott. The church was downtown, just across the street from the State Capitol. Some of the country's best-trained black ministers had preached there. Its membership included many influential professional people from Alabama State University, as well as some folks from the famous nearby private Tuskegee University.

Although Dr. King had the disadvantage of having been in Montgomery only a short time and was still relatively unknown, he had the advantage of not being beholden to the city's white power structure. The local labor leader and another pastor both agreed that the city needed new leadership, and politically King would be the best one to have in charge of the boycott. If he failed, the black city leadership would still be in place and ready to keep things quiet. Dr. King accepted the one-day responsibility. Under his leadership, some fifty thousand people maintained a near-perfect unity and discipline. And they did so not only for a day, but for 382 days! The boycott ended in a favorable U.S. Supreme Court decision that declared Alabama's state and local laws requiring segregation on buses unconstitutional, upholding an earlier ruling of a three-judge U.S. District Court panel.

Although the actual boycott ended in 1956, racial tensions and violence were worse in the years afterward. In 1956 and 1957, after the buses were integrated, the KKK grew and homes and churches were being bombed. While the bus boycott was the biggest news in town for the fifty thousand blacks of Montgomery for more than a year, the citizens had not yet crowned Dr. King the leader and celebrity he later became. One reason may have been that when you are going through a tough struggle day after day, you just say a prayer and follow instructions. Those instructions were repeated at individual churches every Sunday morning, so not all of the people got to see Dr. King at the weekly boycott committee meetings.

Staying off the city buses - where blacks were 75 percent of the daily riders - became a symbol, in my view, of saying, "I won't take injustice anymore. You can have your buses all to yourselves." The irony here is that most of the whites stopped riding the buses also, while the white wives were driving their black housekeepers and cooks between work and home.

As the boycott continued, the bus line was losing money and so was the city, since it received 20 percent of the bus line's weekly profit. The bus drivers who lost their jobs became angry with the drivers who had put blacks off their buses. Blacks of all classes and walks of life came together and worked as a strong unit under Dr. King's leadership, and they were proud to do so. All of this was due to Dr. King's nonviolent leadership and relationship with the people. Everyone believed in him, through some very tough times. No black leader had had such support from the people since the days of Booker T. Washington.

Dr. King's Influence

Dr. King morally influenced the people of Montgomery, the nation, and the world. He led the first successful large-scale, nonviolent movement of civil disobedience in the United States, an idea expounded by Henry David Thoreau. In his first book about the boycott, *Strive Toward Freedom*, Dr. King wrote that when he received the telephone call telling him he had been elected president of a new organization, The MIA, to be in charge of the boycott, and was asked if he would accept, he had less than fifteen minutes to decide. He had to travel across town to the church, where 3,000 to 4,000 people were waiting - including television crews. What would he say? It would be his first speech to the people of Montgomery, both black and white.

I guess when you are in doubt in the South, use the words of Booker T. Washington. King told the crowd, "in spite of the mistreatment that we have confronted, we must not become bitter and end up by hating our white brothers." As Booker T. Washington said, "Let no man pull you so low as to make you hate him." The audience responded enthusiastically. Dr. King elevated the issue of equality into a moral crusade and appealed to the conscience of Montgomery's white citizens and the nation. His successful peaceful protests - using nonviolent tactics even when met with violent opposition - have become a legacy after his death, and his name remains a symbol of the modern civil rights movement. Dr. King's birthday is now celebrated as a national holiday in America, a historic moment acknowledged around the world. What made Dr. King great and well remembered was his conservative message of not hating your enemies and of working to afford opportunities to all.

My thoughts on Dr. King are based on memory and talks with members of my family and friends who are still living in Montgomery. I also read two books several times. I would recommend them both. The first, *The Women Behind the Montgomery Bus Boycott*, was written by my freshman-year English professor at Alabama State, Jo Ann Gibson Robinson, who was also the secretary of the boycott committee and president of the black professional women of Montgomery. The second book is Dr. King's *Stride Toward Freedom*. I also read the Rev. Ralph Abernathy's unpublished thesis on the boycott, which he submitted to Atlanta University.

When many of us think of Dr. King, we focus on his 1963 "I Have A Dream" speech, as though the words in that speech reflect the only dream he had. King, however, was a spiritual leader who had many strongly held beliefs. He expressed some of them in his *Letter from the Birmingham Jail* and in *Where Do We Go From Here?* He expressed his views on education when he said, "The discrimination of the future will not be based on race but on education. Those without education will find no place in our highly sophisticated, technical society." He was absolutely correct.

Unfortunately, in this rush to fight for our own causes and invoke the power of Dr. King, the man's own agenda too often gets tossed aside. A closer look at his life and legacy tell us he had so much more to say than just dreaming. At the age of twenty-six, King received a Ph.D. in systematic theology from Boston University. King's pursuit of higher education exemplified his insight that to fight for your dreams, you must be equipped to do battle. Before the dream can come true, quality education must be offered to every American child-regardless of race.

Today, virtually every group in America that could possibly be discriminated against has fought to become a protected class and complains about injustice. But Dr. King wasn't a complainer. He was a leader who realized that to get to an end, we must first make a commitment to the means. King, in the end, was about "racial freedom, economic justice, and Christian love."

Dr. King's dream remains relevant today. With our present climate of race relations in the country, those who are under the age of fifty may have a little difficulty understanding that just fifty years ago the country's racial landscape was dramatically different. I did not read that in a black studies class: I lived through the era that the notorious Supreme Court case of *Plessy v. Ferguson* created in 1896, and which was not reversed until May 17, 1954 in *Brown v. the Board of Education*, which was only one part of its reach. The Montgomery bus boycott case ended second-class citizenship in transportation in 1956, and more laws were updated during the 1960s.

The challenge today in making Dr. King's dream real is that we still have too many loyal Americans segregated in our hearts and in our thinking about one another. Unfortunately, the law can't make you love yourself in order to love others. The dream today is to overcome racism not only in Alabama and Georgia but all over the country.

Dr. King, in his famous speech during the 1963 march on Washington, envisioned a world where we could live together, where children of every race and color could play together. Our charge is to carry out his dream, not just through tolerance - defined in the Oxford Dictionary as the ability to endure, especially with forbearance, and respect the rights and opinions of others - but also through real understanding of other cultures and social groups. Only then can the legacy of Dr. King be realized.

Eldridge Cleaver

One of the unfortunate consequences of Dr. King's premature death was the emergence of black extremism in place of nonviolence. The Black Panthers were by far the most visible embodiment of this new form of black protest. One of the Panther leaders was an intriguing character named Leroy Eldridge Cleaver. He is famous both for his criminal activities as a Panther leader and for his ideological conversion to Christianity and political conversion to the Republican Party. Cleaver died in 1997, and his passing at age sixty-two made for front-page news. The obituaries focused on what appeared to be a stunning paradox: a former Black Panther leader who died "a true conservative." Yet this ideological journey is not as great as one might expect. In fact, it was an entirely natural one.

Cleaver was born in 1935 in Wabbaseka, Arkansas. His father was a dining car waiter and musician, and his mother was an elementary school teacher. Eldridge Cleaver was a bright student, but he spent most of his teenage years in prison. Upon his release, Cleaver joined the Black Panther Party in 1966 with a mission of protecting the community and its children. His work with the Panthers gave constructive focus to his life. Mr. Cleaver became nationally known as the fiery spokesman for the Black Panther Party, the organization that became famous for wearing black garb, carrying guns, and attacking police.

The Black Panthers were founded by Huey Newton in 1966 to carry out armed resistance to perceived white oppression. The Panthers engaged in numerous confrontations with white police officers, often resulting in the death of officers and Panthers. The organization symbolized the black shift away from the integrationist nonviolence of Dr. King toward violent protest and Black Nationalism. Although the Panthers eventually rejected Black Nationalism in favor of a more universal socialism, they were forever associated in the public's mind with black power, violence, and anti-white sentiment.

Although the violence of the Black Panthers was completely counter to King's nonviolent resistance, the Panthers did share at least one conservative foundation: they believed that blacks would not be saved by government benevolence but by standing up on their own. Panther leaders made it clear they did not approve of the burgeoning welfare state. Mr. Cleaver's position was that liberal electoral politics were bankrupt and could not solve the problems of poverty, racism and oppression. Rather, liberal policies were weakening the black community and forcing blacks into a new servitude.

In order to foster self-reliance, the Black Panthers ran their own community projects, giving free breakfasts to black children, and offered free health clinics and testing for sickle cell anemia. One could argue that the Panthers were the first black organization to attack the whole concept of a welfare state. During his time with the Panthers, Eldridge Cleaver participated in many of the hotly controversial activities of the panthers and, after a shootout with police, jumped bail and fled to Algeria in 1968. In 1974 he spent a year living covertly in France, during which time he became a born-again Christian. In 1975 he returned to the United States where he was sentenced to probation for assault.

Over the course of his life, Mr. Cleaver spent years in prison, was addicted to drugs, was a self-proclaimed rapist, an ideological communist, and a proponent of Black Nationalism. That he spent the last few decades of his life as a born-again Christian - and eventually a Mormon - and a conservative Republican, makes his one of the most fascinating stories of the civil rights era. His final contribution was as a diversity consultant, teaching nonviolence and the brotherhood of man at the University of La Verne in California up until shortly before his death in 1998.

Historians and writers face a daunting challenge when studying Eldridge Cleaver. His story is not as clear-cut as those Black Panthers who lived and died as members of the violent protest movement. He is a testament to the human ability to change. Yet throughout all of his many personal metamorphoses, he continued to believe that blacks should stand up on their own and fulfill their destinies rather than depend upon white benevolence. In this sense, Mr. Cleaver was always a conservative.

Louis Farrakhan

Another controversial figure whose contribution to race relations has evolved over time is the Muslim minister Louis Farrakhan. As the leader of the Nation of Islam, Minister Farrakhan has advocated black nationalism and separatism for decades. Although his rhetoric has often been harsh, many of his underlying ideas have great potential in strengthening the prospects for black Americans. His advocacy of self-help and religious faith send an important message to black people, especially the young. He has both advocated and worked to enable blacks to take personal responsibility for their lives and help one another reach their potential for positive accomplishments. Farrakhan is a former East Coaster of West Indian heritage who grew up in the Episcopal Church. He was an intelligent student who attended a historically black college. An Episcopal priest and college professor married him. He's a proud father and husband. He was a musician and continues to play the violin.

Farrakhan has worked with black youths who have been in the prison system, and has been successful in bringing them back as model citizens. He is a strong proponent of quality education. The respect for education in the black community once had a long and solid tradition. Today, public education is in a major crisis for black youths. Farrakhan's concern for education puts him solidly in the tradition of black conservatism in that regard.

Unfortunately, Farrakhan's rhetoric of self-help and religious devoutness has long been intermingled with a thoroughly offensive anti-Semitism. Rather like Eldridge Cleaver before him, Farrakhan had a later-life change of heart that has resulted in much good. There was a historic meeting of a group of Orthodox Jewish leaders in 1998 at Farrakhan's Chicago home. The goal appears to have been an interfaith discussion of peace. Rabbi David Weiss, spokesman for the group, said, "The meeting was held to clarify what is a Jew and what our position is to all the nations of the world and specifically what our position is to the Nation of Islam and the reverend honorable Minister Farrakhan."

Farrakhan said he was "purified" by a near-death experience during a recent illness and would spend the rest of his life helping all people, regardless of race or creed. In short, Farrakhan said he had decided to work for peace for all, including Jews. That was an important rhetorical step for him to take. He has since emphasized his change of heart in several other speeches, most notably his farewell speech to the Nation of Islam in Detroit in early 2007.

Farrakhan is not usually viewed as having mainstream views within the black community. But his opinion on the meaning of Hurricane Katrina for the black community was as good as or better than any found in the mainstream press. Speaking in 2005 to a crowd of about a thousand people, including evacuees from New Orleans, at Bethel AME church on the south side of Chicago, Farrakhan said, "just as Democrats and Republicans came together after September 11, 2001, black Americans of all religions must join forces to help hurricane victims. Katrina is our reason."

Few people who are not black realize that 9/11 was largely a white experience. Television coverage of the tragedy in New York showed that most of the victims and most of the heroes were white. In New Orleans, the ratios were reversed. Farrakhan pointed out that Katrina was therefore a much more culturally salient issue for blacks than 9/11 was. He went on to say, "the suffering of Katrina victims has brought black people together in a way that hasn't been seen in a long time." He asked the question, "How much do blacks love one another? It's not enough to send a dollar, some clothes or food, because those are things many of us can part from. What's required is that we open our doors and let our family come in."

This isn't the rhetoric of victimhood we heard so much of from spokespersons for the civil rights movement following Katrina. Nor does it contain echoes of the entitlement mentality that implies that people can be helped simply by giving them goods or money. Farrakhan correctly called on the black community to pull together and help its own by providing the kind of personal help and support that family members are expected to give one another.

This is a smart and positive message that goes way beyond "playing the race card." We should always give credit where it is due. On the meaning of Katrina to the black community and on what needed to be done in the hurricane's aftermath, Farrakhan was way ahead of the crowd. On these matters, leaders in both the black and white communities would do well to listen to him.

Justice Clarence Thomas

One cannot discuss prominent conservative blacks without mentioning Justice Clarence Thomas. He has been a steadfast advocate of conservative principles and a color-blind society for his entire tenure on the U.S. Supreme Court as well as during his work for the Equal Employment Opportunity Commission. In 2006 Clarence Thomas concluded fifteen years on the Supreme Court. While labeled a conservative and, erroneously, anti-black by some, the Justice really lived out the life his grandfather hoped for him during the 1960s civil rights movement, which was about social and economic parity in America and ending legally enforced racial segregation.

In a speech delivered to The American Enterprise Institute in 2001, Justice Thomas was, as always, extremely thought provoking and on target. He made the case that he still suffers some victimization but now has the courage to stand tall and disregard it. In short, he showed a glimpse of a Clarence Thomas many don't know. Justice Thomas told the audience:

> I am going to speak more broadly tonight as a citizen who believes in a civil society, and who is concerned because too many show timidity today precisely when courage is demanded...Judges do not cease to be human beings when they go on the bench. In important cases, it is my humble opinion that finding the right answer is often the least difficult problem. The courage to assert that answer and stand firm in the face of the constant winds of protest and criticism is often much more difficult.[34]

Justice Thomas is frequently labeled a conservative merely because of his position on affirmative action - he's against it - but he more clearly belongs in the conservative camp because of his stance on original intent - he's for it. Original intent is a theory of judicial interpretation scorned by liberals but highly regarded by conservatives. According to the theory, constitutional meaning should be discovered by investigating the intent of the constitutional framers. When disputes arise about the meaning of a certain sentence, clause, or even word in the Constitution, justices should consult the historical record, not current public opinion as the relevant authority. The idea is to free the Constitution from the whims of the crowd or the personal inclinations of the justices. Clarence Thomas has actively defended the doctrine of original intent, and his refusal to bend the constitution to suit current liberal dogma has won him countless enemies on the left.

Clarence Thomas has also showed his conservative credentials by rejecting trendy social science as a basis for constitutional jurisprudence. In the recent Seattle school case, *Parents Involved in Seattle Schools v. Seattle School District No. 1*, Thomas sided with the majority in holding race-based admission policies in a Seattle public school district unconstitutional. In his concurring opinion he stated "The Constitution does not permit race-based government decision making simply because a school district claims a remedial purpose and proceeds in good faith with arguably pure motives." Justice Thomas does not believe the Constitution entrusts powers to conduct

---

[34] Clarence Thomas, *Lee Boyer Lecture,* Presentation Delivered at American Enterprise Institute, 2001.

social engineering to government agencies, least of all to school boards. His distrust of government and his fidelity to the strict meaning of the constitutional text - informed by his pursuit of original intent - frequently lead Justice Thomas to conservative conclusions.

In a rather sharp retort to Justice Breyer, one of the most liberal Supreme Court justices, Thomas said in his concurring opinion in the Seattle case:

> Regardless of what Justice Breyer's goals might be, this Court does not sit to "create a society that includes all Americans" or to solve the problems of "troubled inner city schooling." We are not social engineers. The United States Constitution dictates that local governments cannot make decisions on the basis of race. Consequently, regardless of the perceived negative effects of racial imbalance, I will not defer to legislative majorities where the Constitution forbids it.

It is for his unwillingness to remake American society according the liberal vision that Thomas is ostracized by the left. They find his belief in limited government and his strict constructionist approach to the law a barrier to their social engineering. Specifically, his opposition to the black left's favorite son, affirmative action, has promoted Thomas to public enemy number one. And yet, for the past 17 years Clarence Thomas has faithfully executed his duty to interpret the United States Constitution.

As a conservative black myself, I can only hope Justice Thomas' vision of a color-blind America wins over his fellow justices.

Colin Powell and Condoleezza Rice

Another prominent black who has embraced elements of conservatism is Colin Powell. Powell was, for a time, one of the most recognized black political figures in the world. His public approval ratings as Chairman of the Joint Chiefs of Staff were sky-high after the first Gulf War in 1991, and when he briefly considered running for president in 1996 he received support from a broad cross section of America. As Secretary of State under President George W. Bush, he earned the respect of nearly all the world leaders with whom he dealt. When Mr. Powell received the Ronald Reagan Freedom Award in 1993, Mr. Reagan said, "I came to know him as someone I could rely on as a steady and wise adviser. He is a man of the highest integrity, intelligence, and skill."

Growing up in Alabama, I can remember when most folks, blacks in particular, would have been very proud to see the appointment of the first black U.S. Secretary of State. Yet the enthusiasm among black leaders was muted, to say the least, when the appointment came. And when Mr. Powell did not attend the United Nations conference on racism in South Africa in 2001, a small group of American blacks and whites actually called for his resignation. They thought he should have attended because, as a black American, he would have made a significant difference. We'll never know, because the conference ended up being more about attempting to embarrass Israel and the United States than seeking real solutions to global racism.

Historians and psychologists may someday explain why many blacks and some whites find it too difficult to acknowledge black Republicans as authentic role models for black youth and blacks in general. The most recent example is President Bush's appointment of Dr. Condoleezza Rice to the position of Secretary of State, replacing Colin Powell as the second black to hold that office and the first black female to do so.

Since race, class, and diversity still matter in the United States and are the highest priorities for the nation's black leaders, the news of this appointment should have been a positive and historic story in most dailies and the subject of great acclaim by most black columnists. Instead, black leaders and writers condemned Rice as not being an authentic role model for blacks. According to John McWhorter in his 2003 book, *Authentically Black*, thinking people have drifted away from common sense on this issue during the past few decades. McWhorter argues that blacks are passing down the badge of victimization from one generation to the next and thus trapping themselves in chronic poverty and underachievement. When some blacks, such as Rice, break out of the victimhood caricature, the entire charade of victimization is threatened. The backlash against Rice therefore must be understood as the bitter response of those who want to "keep whites on the hook" against one who has chosen self-determination. McWhorter also roundly condemns the reparations hustlers who seem intent on trying to line their pockets rather than empowering their people.

There is no need for me to recount the many personal attacks on Dr. Rice, which were meant to seriously damage her historical image and destroy her credibility as a representative of black aspirations. This treatment was exceedingly perverse in light of Dr. Rice's contributions as a scholar at Stanford University and more recently as National Security

Advisor. One of the most accomplished and successful black Americans of the past quarter-century was used as a piñata by leftist race panderers bent on destroying an alternative image of success for black Americans. It was a disgraceful spectacle.

Dr. Rice deserved much better. She was born in Birmingham, Alabama, on November 14, 1954. An only child, she was home-schooled for her first year, took ballet lessons, and started studying piano at age three. Her mother, a schoolteacher and an accomplished musician, named her Condoleezza from an Italian musical term - con dolcezza - meaning "with sweetness." When Condoleezza was eleven, the family moved to Tuscaloosa, Alabama. Her father, John, was a pastor and educator who was offered the position of Dean at Stillman College - the same school his own father had attended. After three years at Stillman, he was offered a position as assistant director of admissions at the University of Denver.

While a senior in high school, Condoleezza enrolled at the University of Denver. At nineteen, she graduated cum laude and was invited to join Phi Beta Kappa. She received a master's degree from Notre Dame and returned to Denver, receiving a doctorate in political science in 1981. After her doctorate, Stanford University offered her a research fellowship at its Center for International Security and Arms Control.

After a few months as a research fellow, she became an assistant professor. In 1987, she advanced to associate professor. When Brent Scowcroft became the National Security Advisor for George H. W. Bush, he asked Rice to take a two-year leave of absence to work with him. In 1993, she became a full professor at Stanford. Just a few months later, the university's president asked her to become the school's provost - making her the first black to hold the position, and she managed a $1.5 billion budget. She met George W. Bush in 1995 while he was governor of Texas. Her knowledge of sports and foreign policy impressed him.

Condoleezza Rice is one of a rising cadre of black leaders who are breaking new ground for the race. We should be proud of her accomplishments and encourage our children and grandchildren to embrace her as a role model.

Tiger Woods

Although Tiger Woods has avoided political statements during the course of his career, he embodies the virtues of black conservatism. He has pursued excellence, eschewed special privilege on account of his race, and sought to achieve greatness in an arena of fierce competition. That he both became the greatest young golfer of his generation and still achieved enough academically to gain acceptance to Stanford University is a testimony to his uncompromising work ethic.

Tiger Woods decided early in his life that he would not embrace an identity as a victim. This did not mean that he was naively unaware of the realities of racism. During Mr. Woods' initial interviews after leaving college to become a professional golfer, he referred to golf courses where, only a short time ago, he could not play because of his color. Three years later, he was being hailed as the eight-hundred-pound giant of sports who could end gender or racial discrimination resulting from age-old customs of "white male privilege."

Without a doubt, black Americans continue to be stars on the world's stage of sports since the days of Jackie Robinson, the baseball star, and Joe Louis in the boxing ring. However, on April 10, 2005, at the Masters tournament in Augusta, Georgia, Tiger Woods truly raised the bar for sports achievement.

Let me admit that I am partisan when talking about golf. While many today describe golf as a middle-class sport, I and many other southern boys were introduced to the game as caddies during our high school and college days. There were two jobs we southern blacks didn't have to compete with white boys for: picking cotton and being a caddy. One could earn $1.25 for five hours on the golf course and $2 for picking cotton from sunup to sundown. I chose golf whenever I could. As a result, I learned more about a game I enjoyed playing. No, they did not allow us to play on the course at any time, but we could swing the clubs, and we played on hard dirt on our school playgrounds after school and on weekends.

I have an autographed picture of Tiger Woods hanging on my wall, but I pay more attention to a full-page ad featuring Tiger that reads, "Do you see opportunities when others don't?" It then reads, "High performance. Delivered." I have found some life lessons in understanding the game of golf. It tells you a lot about a person's character and determination, as well as how he or she plays a gentleman's game. Golf was once played in shirt and tie, and it still is on some courses. Golf has a unique difference from most sports. You are not playing against a rival, but instead playing against yourself and the course. It is what many describe as a mind game. I have found that if you believe you can make a shot, most of the time you will.

Tiger fired his first pro coach, and many said that he was foolish to do so because they believed Tiger's coach was responsible for his success. The truth, however, was that Tiger's father was the real spring of Tiger's competitive spirit and quiet determination. Tiger's self confidence, fueled by his father, enabled him to walk away from his coach in order to reach an even higher level of play. His old coach asked Tiger, why change your swing in the middle of success? Tiger, however, was not playing to be just a good golfer; he wanted to be the best he could become.

The life lesson to be learned from Tiger and his golf mission is to never stop challenging yourself to do better, and don't measure yourself against someone else. We all have different talents. Tiger is earning more money than any golfer in history, yet he is not letting money be his driving force. Tiger's commitment to his charitable foundation is also laudable, as his organization works to teach young children the game of golf regardless of whether they can afford to play the sport today. With perseverance, these young people might well be able to excel in the sport tomorrow.

Black Role Models

There are countless other less well known, but equally impressive conservative blacks I have had the honor of knowing over the years. My friend, Rev. William Winston, exemplifies the best of the conservative tradition. A former fighter pilot in the US Air Force, Rev. Winston went on to a successful career with IBM before leaving the corporate world to start a church. He founded Living Word Christian Center in Forest Park, Illinois with little more than hard work and a vision of empowering people.

Living Word Christian Center is now a 15,000 member church and it has since launched the Bible Training Center, a School of Ministry and Mission, and the Living Word Christian Academy. Pastor Winston also hosts the Believer's Walk of Faith television and radio broadcast which reaches an audience of over 80 million.

Pastor Winston recognized that his parishioners needed more than spiritual instruction, they needed life instruction. He therefore started the Joseph School of Business to teach people entrepreneurial skills and the Forest Park Plaza Shopping Center where his congregants could build their work skills and learn vital business management strategies. An entrepreneur himself, Pastor Winston has taught hundreds of eager young business owners how to launch a successful enterprise.

Pastor Winston founded the Joseph Center for Business Development and sits on the board of the New Covenant Community Bank. He believes that when presented with a vision and equipped with basic business skills, blacks can transform their own communities into thriving economic powerhouses. Pastor Winston is one of a growing crowd of entrepreneurs leading the black community away from dependence on government and into a new era of self-help and community redevelopment.

Another personal friend of mine who represents the fulfillment of the conservative vision is Dr. Carol M. Swain. As the biography on her website states:

> Dr. Swain has lived the American Dream. From a family of twelve children suffering from extreme rural poverty in Bedford, Virginia, she has risen to professor in the halls of Vanderbilt University. Through her nonprofit educational organization, The Veritas Institute, she now works to restore the hope of the American dream: that individuals can rise above the circumstances of their birth, that opposing groups can listen to each other and benefit from civil dialogue, and that ordinary people can have a voice.[35]

Instead of harboring bitterness and anger against American society, Dr. Swain has worked actively to bring reconciliation and healing between blacks and whites. She has authored award-winning books including *Black Faces, Black Interests: The Representation of African Americans in Congress* (Harvard University Press, 1993, 1995: reprinted University Press of America, 2006), which won the Woodrow Wilson prize for the best book published in the U. S. on government, politics, or international affairs in 1994, and was cited by U.S. Supreme Court Justice Anthony Kennedy in *Johnson v. DeGrandy*, (1994) and twice by Justice Sandra Day O' Connor in *Georgia V. Ashcroft*, (2003).

Professor Swain pursued education with a passion, earning a B.A. from Roanoke College, an M.A. from Virginia Polytechnic Institute and State University, a Ph.D. from The University of North Carolina at Chapel Hill, and most recently a M.L.S. from Yale Law School. Dr. Swain is currently Professor of Political Science and Professor of Law at Vanderbilt University and formerly taught at Princeton University. Her love of learning

---

[35] www.carolmswain.net/bio.html

is matched only by her zeal for teaching. Dr. Swain is an incredible role model to young black students who wonder just how far a sharp mind and a hunger for knowledge can take them.

All of the individuals I have mentioned in this chapter have embraced conservative values in their own personal lives, not just in the political sphere. Through a combination of hard work, perseverance, devotion to education, and self-confidence they have accomplished breathtaking achievements. Every black parent has the option of teaching their children to prize these virtues. The alternative is to inculcate a sense of entitlement, victimization and bitterness at America.

The first option opens the doors to amazing opportunities; the second option ensures lifelong dependency and despair. Black parents and teachers should hold up Tiger Woods, Colin Powell, Condoleezza Rice, Bill Cosby and other successful, self-made blacks as role models. As racism continues to lose its power in the United States, blacks should embrace the conservative values that gave us strength to overcome the indignity of slavery and the crippling effects of Jim Crow. That same strength will now empower us to secure for ourselves economic independence, prosperity and the freedom to choose our destiny.

Chapter 8

Contemporary Issues

Black conservatism is not tied to a single political party. Neither does black conservatism have a ten-point agenda or doctrinal statement. As I mentioned in the introduction to this book, black conservatism is a way of looking at the social order that highlights the inherent dignity and freedom of individuals and the responsibility that all people have to achieve to their full potential. This chapter contains one black conservative's take on a range of hot button issues and demonstrates how true conservatism is the answer to today's problems for blacks and whites alike.

Affirmative Action

The year 2004 marked the fortieth anniversary of the Civil Rights Act, a fantastic piece of legislation that ended segregation of public facilities and outlawed discrimination in hiring. The Act helped bring to an end a long and disgraceful period in American history when many states practiced legally enforced segregation and discrimination. These policies made a mockery of the freedom supposedly won by blacks after the Civil War and passage of the Thirteenth, Fourteenth and Fifteenth Amendments to the Constitution.

Republicans in the years following the Civil War rightly bear much of the blame for the subsequent legal segregation and blatant discrimination. They betrayed blacks in the South by pulling federal troops out too soon, which allowed southern whites to impose mandatory segregation laws. The decades following Reconstruction were the lowest point in the history of blacks in America.

Republicans redeemed themselves somewhat in 1964 by providing the votes needed to pass the Civil Rights Act. Though Democrats today spin it as a Democratic initiative, more Democrats than Republicans voted against the Civil Rights Act. Democrats in the Senate voted 46 for, 21 against, while Republicans voted 27 for and only 6 against. In the House, Democrats voted 152 for and 96 against, while Republicans voted 138 for and only 34 against.

The Civil Rights Act's biggest contribution was ending legal segregation in public facilities and outlawing discrimination in hiring. Soon thereafter affirmative action began as a remedy for discrimination against nonwhites. Affirmative action started by setting aside a percentage of federal contracts for minorities and later expanded to include corporate hiring and college admissions. When white women began qualifying for affirmative action benefits, it changed from a racial remedy into a more vague and general liberal protest movement against business. There is no evidence it is helping blacks get ahead today.

I believe strongly in the original concept of affirmative action: to increase the pool of candidates for job selection, contracts, and admission to colleges without regard to color, race, or sex - in short, first class citizenship. I utterly deny that we are originally, or naturally, or practically, or in any way or in any important sense inferior to anybody on this globe.

Affirmative action targets the wrong problem in the wrong way. In the early 1960s, I was one of three African-American office boys employed by a national real estate developer in New York City's Rockefeller Center area. In those days, even office boys were considered part of the corporate world and were expected to act and dress the part. Thus, we had our three-piece suits and attaché cases containing our lunches, a newspaper, and usually a textbook. Most of us were also attending college in the evenings. I was a student at New York University, having previously attended Alabama State College in Montgomery. Since I was already inside the corporate door, newly established affirmative action programs served to change my title from office boy to office manager. I got an increase in pay, but had the same responsibilities.

What I lacked was affirmative opportunity - the ability to take on a more important role at the firm. That opportunity came after the 1960s riots, when the company saw me as an asset for dealing with lily-white trade labor unions. I became director of labor relations and helped integrate the workforce. It was only when I could help the company's bottom line that I received a real opportunity to move up in the hierarchy. I would agree that affirmative action over the past thirty-plus years has been a successful outreach strategy for hiring minorities and women. But it's an idea that has run its course. Women and minorities have been hired, but they haven't moved up the ladder. It's time to focus less on affirmative action and more on affirmative opportunity, at least for blacks.

For example, in 1990 black females held only 6 percent of middle management jobs, while black males held only 5 percent. This was after three decades of affirmative action. Can this really be called a success? We have to stop playing the numbers game in terms of simply hiring people. The sheer demand for workers means minorities are already being hired. The real question is how much opportunity is there for upward mobility once you're in the door.

Affirmative action should be revisited because it has been perverted from its original intent of addressing legitimate past grievances. The federal government has attempted to establish particular hiring patterns instead of equality of opportunity. Now, does the fact that I want to change affirmative action mean that I believe racism has disappeared? An emphatic no! However, affirmative action has become the public policy equivalent of an earthquake, splitting the country and shaking apart friendships, communities, businesses, and political parties. Yet despite these very real problems it has caused, many blacks are afraid to revisit the affirmative action debate.

In 1984, Thomas Sowell called for this kind of debate in his book, *Civil Rights: Rhetoric or Reality?* Twenty years earlier, U.S. Sen. Daniel Patrick Moynihan had called for such a debate in his report on the disintegration of the black family. We are still awaiting that debate, and it is urgently needed, for only a debate over the real purpose of affirmative action can allow us to move on to a push for affirmative opportunity.

Many in the black community argue that even though affirmative action is harmful to American democracy, blacks must continue to push for it because whites are still using it. On September 30, 2005, for example, the *Chicago Sun-Times* ran an insightful letter by James Thindwa on how the Bush administration opposed affirmative action for blacks but used cronyism and discrimination to elevate incompetent whites to high positions at FEMA. However, the Bush administration's hypocrisy cannot be used to justify affirmative action.

Affirmative action may have been necessary to overcome discrimination when it was first introduced, but it has run its course. Attempts to avoid, evade, and game racial preference programs are what drove them to become rigid quotas. Worse, these programs are often rightly accused of putting "who you know" ahead of "what can you do?" as Chicago's ongoing struggle with fronts and shams in its purchasing set-aside programs demonstrates.

Misbehavior by white politicians cannot be prevented or reduced by imposing racial and gender preferences, if ever it was. Rehashing old debates about affirmative action diverts attention from improving schools and the work habits of our young people and expanding the economic resources of the black community. This is why black conservatives, myself included, can comfortably condemn cronyism, discrimination, *and* affirmative action.

We must recognize that cronyism and discrimination are wrong regardless of the color of the recipient. The 1995 *Adarand v. Pena* Supreme Court case involved a federal affirmative action policy administered in Colorado that awarded 1.5 percent bonuses to prime contractors who subcontract work to "disadvantaged" business people. Racial minorities were perceived to meet such qualifications if they were certified by the Small Business Administration. Adarand, a white contractor, submitted the lowest bid to the prime contractor, but Frank Gonzales, a minority contractor, got the contract. Although the district court and court of appeals upheld Colorado's decision to award Gonzales the contract, the Supreme Court overturned the decision and stated that the government must have a "compelling interest" to establish race conscious policies. These policies must then be subject to "strict scrutiny" to determine whether or not the compelling interest is being met.

Many civil rights leaders believed the Supreme Court decision would set back the gains made by minorities and blacks. They were wrong. The meaning of the term "affirmative action" has been stretched far beyond its initial purpose. Today, the term means different things to different groups. It is still being held up as one of the Ten Commandments for blacks if they want to enjoy the American dream. That is a misplaced vision.

Too many blacks believe, incorrectly, that they can succeed only with the help of affirmative action. Such an attitude is an insult to all of the blacks that succeeded against great odds long before affirmative action. There are other side-effects not usually mentioned in the present debate, which were highlighted in Justice Clarence Thomas' comments on the case. He stated, "Government cannot make us equal; it can only recognize, respect and protect us equally before the law," and "These programs stamp minorities with a badge of inferiority and may cause them to develop dependencies or to adopt an attitude that they are entitled to preferences."

In the 1950s and '60s, there were few blacks employed at the highest levels of the public or private sectors. Today we have more, but they are bumping up against an invisible ceiling blocking advancement. When Hobart Taylor Jr., a black attorney, first used the term affirmative action in a conversation with President John F. Kennedy, the meaning was clear and mutually understood. It was to be a hiring, recruitment, and training remedy to help ensure equal opportunity to get through the door and equal treatment thereafter.

That was over 40 years ago. Today, the problem is not so much getting hired as it is being promoted beyond that invisible ceiling. The ceiling is invisible because the height of the ceiling depends on the ethics or morality of senior management. We need another remedy to fight racial discrimination and to ensure affirmative opportunity for all. I would suggest to CEOs that senior management does not need another diversity seminar, but a seminar on ethics and values. A major problem is fear and prejudice generated from the top, not ethnic differences among associates.

Sooner or later, the affirmative action consultants will have the courage to acknowledge the wisdom in Supreme Court Justice Clarence Thomas' statement, "Government cannot make us equal; it can only recognize, respect, and protect us equally before the law."

Today the term "affirmative action" is rarely defined. It has become little more than a slogan to rally black support for the Democratic Party. Whatever its merits and problems, affirmative action has run its course. It no longer deserves to be the focus of attention by blacks. President George W. Bush, like his father and President Reagan before them, understands the difference between guaranteeing equal rights and using government programs in a futile attempt to make people equal. He has not tried to "turn the clock back on civil rights," and his position on the issue deserves a much more balanced view by blacks and civil rights advocates.

College Admissions

Controversy over affirmative action and its relationship to education was rekindled by the U.S. Supreme Court's split decision on the subject in 2003. The cases *Gratz v. Bollinger* and *Grutter v. Bollinger* ended affirmative action at the undergraduate level but perpetuated the use of race in law school admissions. Some folks say Justice Sandra Day O'Connor's swing vote, upholding the law school's narrowly tailored affirmative action program, was the right decision. Others think she only delayed the inevitable - the removal of any kind of government-mandated preference.

After all, she did reject the undergraduate school's point system, as did Justice Clarence Thomas.

The present discussion of affirmative action in college admissions is not about the same thing we discussed in the 1960s. Forty years ago, affirmative action was a remedy meant to ensure individual equal opportunity in hiring, recruiting, training, and bidding for contracts in the marketplace. During today's debate, we hardly hear the terms "civil rights" or "individual equal opportunity." What's important now are "equal group results" and college admissions programs ensuring that a particular number of people of each racial group (and they are rather oddly defined by government policy) gets admitted to the schools. Civil rights and equal opportunity morphed into affirmative action, and now that has become a push for "diversity."

Since the court decision, I've discussed the issue on television news broadcasts and talk radio shows. I've also talked to many college students about it. Within the first minute in these conversations, the discussion turns to racism, white guilt, victimization, and preferences - nothing about whether students are actually equipped to compete and graduate. But the number one civil rights issue today is - or at least should be - quality education. Racism is endemic in American culture, and the best tool for handling it is education.

Many black students don't have the motivation and persistence of Dr. Martin Luther King Jr., who finished high school at age fifteen, college at nineteen, and had a doctorate by the time he was twenty six. He studied for years before trying to save the world. He was as well prepared for that ambitious mission as a person could hope to be at that young age.

What Justice O'Connor didn't say strongly enough, perhaps, is that America's public school system is not equipping all children - and blacks in particular - to graduate and meet college enrollment requirements. This is where we should focus our attention, our energies, and our efforts, so that in 25 years all students will be equipped to take advantage of the opportunities for higher education this nation affords.

Welfare Reform

Our emphasis should be on equality of opportunity, not equality of results. That means creating a system in which talent and hard work are rewarded regardless of all other considerations, and in which individuals are thereby encouraged to rely on their own efforts and the help of their families.

I believe that the 1990s welfare reform was a real blessing for low-income families and the truly disadvantaged. The reform, led by Republicans, was guided by one principle: to help those in extreme need who are not able to help themselves and to encourage those who could help themselves to do so. The principle behind it was that help should be given only through a process that perpetuates an attitude of self-reliance rather than creating a cycle of dependency or a new middle class establishment of poverty professionals.

It's no accident that the Family Support Act of 1988, with its claims of dramatic reform, did not go nearly far enough. After sixty years the welfare system had developed a nationwide welfare industry, and it was not in that industry's best interest that welfare "as we know it" truly disappear. The Republicans' Personal Responsibility Act of 1996 offered the foundation for true reform. Key elements were to stop penalizing poor people for being married and working, to stop giving incentives for males to leave the house, and to make welfare a mutual obligation between government and the recipient. Young men and women can no longer ignore personal responsibility. Recipients have to work or go to school in order to continue to receive their welfare benefits.

Although liberals, addicted to the welfare state, predicted massive increases in poverty would result from the 1996 welfare reform, welfare programs, it turns out, do not seem to have any appreciable impact on poverty levels. The federal government - which runs more than seventy five interrelated and overlapping programs - turned over management of those programs to the states. The states have proven to be far more effective managers of these programs. Both the number of people currently on the welfare rolls and the amount of money spent on welfare have declined since 1996. For example, in 1996 Illinois had over 600,000 people receiving Temporary Assistance to Needy Families (TANF). By adding work requirements, time limits and family cap provisions, Illinois was able to bring that number down to less than 97,000 in 2006.[36] Under the reform, states now receive grants from the federal government (Illinois received nearly $586M in 2006) but must administer the programs themselves. Remarkably, the overall poverty rate in Illinois actually fell from 12 percent

---

[36] Gary MacDougal and Dane Wendell, *Welfare Reform After Ten Years: A State-by-State Analysis* (Chicago, IL: The Heartland Institute, 2008).

to 10 percent from 1996 to 2000 even as welfare expenditures were dramatically reduced.

Welfare reform has changed the structure of poverty remediation very much for the better, but we have yet to see the full results of this reform, as that will be embodied in the next generation of our children. And with the nation's education system still in a wretched state, it is unlikely that welfare reform alone will be able to turn things around completely. However, at least it is no longer a powerful social curse sending another generation to drugs, jail, and death.

Immigration Reform

Immigration is an important topic for blacks, and the past and present black leadership has failed to represent our real interests in the discussion. Immigration has become the new "third rail" of politics, even hotter than the traditional hot-button topics of abortion and affirmative action. In fact, the *Wall Street Journal*, in a 2006 editorial, said the most critical mail it received from readers, by far, concerns the issue of immigration. For the record, the *Journal* supports very open immigration policies. In the past, blacks marched, then voted, and the results were the 1964 Civil Rights Act and the 1965 Voting Rights Act. Recently, I have been hearing from Hispanic groups the slogan, "Today we march, tomorrow we vote."

The Immigration Reform and Control Act of 1986 combined amnesty for three million illegal immigrants with a promise of tougher enforcement, particularly against employers. The amnesty was delivered, but the promise of tougher enforcement of immigration laws never materialized. Corporate America found a need for more low-cost labor to meet the demands of global competition and a growing economy, and tougher rules never materialized; they just slid off the plate politically.

According to some critics of lax recent immigration enforcement policies, most of these illegals are poor, uneducated, and speak only Spanish. Be that as it may, if twelve million illegal immigrants were to leave the country, the results would be economically disastrous. Although currently unemployed and low-income workers would benefit some because more jobs would be available, labor costs would increase and be passed on to the consumer. This would have a negative effect on consumers, and the poor in particular. The U.S. government would also lose out on money that many illegal immigrants contribute to Medicare and Social Security, even though they are unable to collect benefits due to their age or lack of legal status.

Immigration is a "black issue" because of the economics of labor. Labor is not exempt from the laws of supply and demand. Immigration increases the supply of labor, but generally not the number of jobs. When immigration has increased in the past, it was clearly not in the best interest of most black Americans and other nonwhites, who found themselves competing with low-cost immigrant labor for entry level jobs and other low-wage and less desirable employment.

There is a lot of heated rhetoric going around, but to get a better understanding of what immigration brings to the table of American citizens and its socioeconomic impact, one should look at the history of black Americans and immigration. One of the basic facts of American history that is not widely discussed is the nation's longstanding preference for immigrant labor as opposed to trained and employable native-born black Americans. The Chinese, for example, were kept out of the country by law until the high demand for low-cost labor to build the railroads on the West Coast overcame racist objections. Immigrant labor, beginning with those coming from European countries but extending eventually to the Chinese, was preferred over employment of blacks who were already here. Most of these immigrants spoke no English, but they largely came from the European countries that white America had immigrated from. Blacks were the residual labor pool, never able to enjoy the benefits of full employment except in times of war, when the white immigrant labor supply was not available.

Booker T. Washington, in his famous 1895 Atlanta Exposition speech, pleaded with corporate America and politicians to use the black and white labor supply of the South to work in their new factories rather than use European immigrants:

> Cast down your bucket among the eight millions of Negroes whose habits you know, whose fidelity and love you have tested in days when to have proved treacherous meant the ruin of your firesides. Cast down your bucket among these people who have, without strikes and labor wars, tilled your fields, cleared your forests, builded your railroads and cities, and brought forth treasures from the bowels of the earth, and helped make possible this magnificent representation of the progress of the South.

Few listened.

There were efforts made by the federal government to send black Americans out of the country after the Civil War, just as some propose to send Latinos "back home" today. It did not work with blacks. Thus the experience of blacks in America can be recalled in order to contribute some valid history to today's immigration debate. The present debate includes many of the same elements of discrimination and racism that blacks experienced from the time of the Emancipation Proclamation through the era of the Civil Rights Movement and still endure in the current Affirmative Action era. Immigration has always uncovered some form of discrimination or racism, and this present debate is no exception.

Now, interestingly enough, we are beginning to hear comments like, "Blacks and whites will have to band together to protect our country from the immigrants." And unfortunately, I have to admit that some blacks are buying into this. The solution, however, is not to turn back immigrants who have come to this country to work hard. It is in equipping native blacks with the skills and attitudes to compete with immigrants. At the turn of the twentieth century, Booker T. Washington was the largest black employer of educated blacks in the country. He realized that he had to find a solution to the problem of unskilled blacks falling behind due to immigration. In a 1912 speech before the National Negro Business League in Chicago he said the following:

> Now is the time - not in some far - off future, but now is the time - for us as a race to prove to the world that in a state of freedom, we have the ability and inclination to do our part in owning, developing, manufacturing, and trading in the natural resources of our country. If the Italians and the Greeks can come to this country, strangers to our language and civilization and within a few years gain wealth and independence by trading in fruits, the Negro can do the same thing.

Unfortunately, Washington died three years later, and the black leadership turned its focus from economics to politics and racial integration, important issues to be sure, but as Washington noted, economic independence remains the essential foundation for personal and group success.

If the nation's black leadership had followed Washington's guidance, it would have asked two questions: How did the European immigrants escape the ghettos so soon after they arrived? and what is the chief cause of blacks' economic inequality? One response appears in J. Owens Smith's book, *The Politics of Racial Inequality* (1987). He wrote:

> Public policies that grant or deny groups the liberty to take advantage of a wide range of economic opportunities that exist within society's income redistribution system become the primary reasons why more blacks and Hispanics have not been able to escape the slums in large numbers. The federal government has historically refused to offer them the same system of protection to acquire property and to pursue a wide range of economic opportunities, as it did for European immigrants.

I understand this, and I believe that Washington understood that point very well. If, however, Washington's advice had been taken, the next twenty years would have found the number of blacks with low skills on the decline in spite of intimidation, and the prosperity of blacks in general would have increased greatly. Washington knew the key was to learn from the successes of others and to recognize that government can only set in place the opportunity for success; it cannot make people prosperous and self-reliant. (That is a lesson we also learned from the disastrous failure of the welfare system and the success of welfare reform.) If you make a product that other people want and value, Washington said again and again, they will have no choice but to buy it from you, to hire you, to begin treating you as their equal.

Immigration currently hurts blacks because welfare policies, combined with a legacy of slavery and institutionalized discrimination, drove men out of the home and weakened the family structure, and labor unions kept blacks from moving up within the trades. The unintended consequence of welfare was to create a people dependent on the charity of others, deprived of role models, and with few assets. When such people find and hold jobs, they tend to be low paying and insecure ones. Of course such people are vulnerable to competition from immigrants. They are trying to live their lives working jobs that are meant only to be steps at the bottom of career ladders.

We should stop and ask ourselves, then, what role the labor movement has had in the recent rush to out source manufacturing and to employ undocumented workers. Has organized labor helped or hurt the prospects of the less skilled and less educated, and those subject to discrimination because of where they live or the color of their skin? In driving up the cost of hiring domestic workers, organized labor has actually encouraged businesses to look elsewhere for their labor supply. Instead of remaining competitive, American union labor is now extremely expensive relative to other sources of labor. Labor unions may end up completely destroying their own livelihoods by focusing too much on increasing wages and too little on improving their competitiveness and efficiency.

The United States of America is still a country that boldly welcomes refugees from other countries, promises that hard work is rewarded, and believes safety and prosperity can be earned here. We must, as a nation, remain open to legal immigration, without discrimination, while protecting ourselves from criminals and terrorists. But at the same time, we must help our vulnerable native populations achieve the American Dream too, by giving them the skills they need to compete with immigrants for good jobs.

Health Scares and Energy Costs

In 2004, the Bush administration proposed dramatic reductions in sulfur dioxide, nitrogen oxides, and mercury from power plants. The recommendations went well beyond the suggestions by actual health and environmental experts at the Mercatus Center, the Cato Institute, the American Enterprise Institute, and other respected think tanks. The danger of such proposals is that by trying to reduce emissions too quickly we risk incurring social costs that far outweigh the small, and often times hypothetical, health benefits we are pursuing.

The administration tried to soften the blow by offering to allow emission trading, similar to the successful program used to reduce sulfur emissions. Emission trading means companies with high costs of reducing emissions can buy emission permits from those with low reduction costs, meaning the required reduction takes place at the lowest cost. It's a good policy, although in this case it was being used to reduce costs that were unnecessarily imposed by government in the first place.

Even though the government ended up passing the Clean Air Mercury Rule in 2005 - making the United States the first country in the world to regulate mercury emissions from utilities - professional environmental advocates still argue the reductions are not enough. They believe emissions trading allows some polluters to continue to pollute, harming their neighbors.

According to the Environmental Protection Agency, however, mercury emissions and their presence in the air are strongly trending downward (as are all other pollutants), and are expected to keep falling due to technological change and implementation of current standards. Furthermore, most of the mercury in the air and entering the Great Lakes today comes either from natural sources or from China and other third world countries that burn coal without any emissions control. More strict standards on power plants here in the U.S. obviously will have no effect on those sources, and consequently have little effect on air or water quality.

Scientists also do not believe there is any hard evidence that eating fish and breathing current ambient levels of mercury pose a health threat, even to children and pregnant women. So why have environmentalists called for steep reductions in mercury and other power plant emissions? By demanding unreasonable reductions in mercury, they hope to discourage the use of coal and eventually other fossil fuels (oil and natural gas), which they think will lead either to a non-industrial utopia where most of us are poor but enjoy ourselves, or to a hyper evolved sci-fi economy where windmills, solar panels, and hydrogen fuel cells generate all the power we need without a smokestack in sight. In reality, neither option is realistic.

What is most likely to happen - indeed, what environmentalists expect will happen - is that energy prices will skyrocket, economic growth will slow, and unemployment will rise. It is undeniable that when this occurs, black and low-income people will be harmed the most. Energy costs take a bigger bite out of the budgets of low income folks than of higher income folks, so higher energy costs are regressive. Higher energy costs also mean slower economic growth and African Americans and the poor are still the "last hired and first fired," hurting us a second time.

And manufacturing is particularly affected by higher energy costs, because manufacturing requires more energy than the service and high-tech sectors of the economy. Higher energy prices therefore make it more difficult for manufacturers in the U.S. to compete with manufacturers located in other countries.

This debate continues to pitch wealthy, white, liberal environmentalists advocating feel good policies, against poor, working class, people of color. The tears many white liberals cry for "poor people" exposed to pollutants are insincere. They are indifferent in this case to the suffering their policies impose on the poor and the black community, just as they are indifferent to the suffering caused by their constant advocacy of higher taxes and more regulation of industry.

One of the reasons I am a conservative is that I have grown tired of seeing white liberals line up against black interests whenever their feel good environmental interests are on the line. Raising blacks' economic level seems more a convenient slogan to gain political power than an actual goal of the white liberal establishment. The recent battle over Mercury regulation is exhibit A.

Price Controls Hurt Blacks

Price controls, a darling of the liberal elite, typically end up hurting poor people once all of their effects are felt. After Hurricane Katrina and Rita in 2005, many Illinois consumers were braced for high energy prices during the winter chill. Trotting out its familiar anti-corporate sentiments, the media blasted Commonwealth Edison for engaging in price gouging. ComEd, however, was not thrilled about the cold weather either. Most people still don't realize it, but since deregulation in 1997, ComEd has been simply an electric delivery company. They don't make electricity anymore. They buy it from power plants owned by somebody else and deliver it, which means they feel the effects of rising fuel prices too.

The Illinois Commerce Commission (ICC) sets the prices ComEd can charge for their services. Over the past ten years energy costs have risen but ComEd's rates have been frozen as part of the deal cut in 1997. It's been a nice holiday for consumers, but a financial nightmare for ComEd, which says the price controls are driving it closer and closer to financial ruin.

The price freeze was scheduled to end in 2007, so naturally ComEd asked the ICC to live up to its side of the agreement by allowing prices to rise. ComEd also asked for delivery fee increases to allow it to recoup the costs of improving the infrastructure over the last several years.

Illinois' political leaders are not excited about being blamed for higher electric bills in an election year. Governor Blagojevich, posing as the consumers' knight in shining armor, loudly opposed the rate increase. No surprise there.

But was a permanent rate freeze realistic? Electricity is perhaps the most vitally important of all public services. We can't expect ComEd to stay on its feet if it is forced to spend more on electricity than it is allowed to charge. California's energy crisis of just a couple years ago showed what happens when politicians impose rigid retail price controls and then tell utilities to buy power in unregulated wholesale markets. The result was blackouts and complete chaos.

A more reasonable strategy would be to allow market forces to set prices, even if it brings higher prices, but then to make sure there are strategies in place to help the state's neediest families get through the pricing changes. We should not expect our elderly and disabled citizens to bear the cost of these higher prices completely on their own. Their burdens are already too great.

There are programs in place already to help those below the poverty line pay their bills. The Low Income Home Energy Assistance Program, for instance, is a federal program that spends billions every year to help low income and fixed income families cover their heating costs. In addition, ComEd has offered to defer billing needy families for several years.

No one likes to pay higher prices for anything, and in normal marketplace circumstances our quest for lower prices results in more efficient markets. But electricity is not a normal marketplace, and politicians pander to our desire for unrealistically low prices. The result threatens the ability of companies like ComEd to do their jobs. And when electric companies can no longer supply energy to consumers, rolling black outs and shortages are the order of the day. The rich who can afford solar panels on their roofs may not notice, but the poor certainly will.

Although blacks have benefitted in the past from government intervention - most significantly in ending school desegregation and Jim Crow style disenfranchisement - the high tax, high regulation government we endure today harms more than helps blacks. If left alone, the free market is the most powerful force for progress and wealth creation known to man. Barriers to the free market inevitably slow economic growth, create unemployment, and inflate prices. Minorities and the poor suffer most from these problems and should hold elected leaders accountable for the consequences of their actions.

Conclusion

In his 1906 essay "An Appeal to Reason on the Race Problem," Kelly Miller wrote:

> Justice, intelligence, thrift and character are virtues of undisputed value, and apply to all men under all conceivable conditions. If the white man, North or South, in dealing with his weaker brother, will apply the principle of justice, and encourage him in the development of intelligence, thrift, and character, he may safely free his mind from the dread of destiny which now occasions such anxious solicitude.[37]

This is where conservatism is essential to blacks' success. Conservatism in this sense speaks not to the conservation of present institutions but instead to the preservation and promulgation of a set of values that we believe are necessary for any individual to attain progress. Washington's book *Up from Slavery*, in which he tells the story of his rise from a poor slave to a great educator and national leader, may be called the manifesto of black conservatism. Washington taught the value of "patience, thrift, good manners, and high morals" in lifting people above their circumstances.

These concepts are not a dream. Washington did it, and countless others have followed him in achieving great things. While political participation is important, black political action during the past century has looked outside the self and relied on white recognition and guilt to help black people better themselves. This makes blacks dependent on others. Looking to oneself, as Washington taught, gives an individual the most power over his destiny.

This does not mean, of course, that a person can entirely determine his own fate, but it does mean that to the extent that it is possible, the individual will achieve all that he or she can. Slavery and the years of Jim Crow

---

[37] Kelly Miller, *An Appeal to Reason on the Race Problem* (Washington, DC: Howard University, 1906).

prevented the ideas of past conservative black leaders from becoming reality at the time. That is a true tragedy. Those ideas, however, have great value today and can enable blacks - and indeed all Americans - to reach their full potential to do good for themselves and for others.

As Kelly Miller notes in discussing Booker T. Washington, "the whole tenor of his teaching has been to persuade his race to place less proportional stress on politics and to concentrate its energies upon things economic and material." Miller correctly observes that Washington's refusal to confront political problems meant that his approach was not the total solution to all that blacks needed at the time, but he acknowledged that Washington's philosophy was an essential half of the program for the improvement of blacks' lot in life.

Commenting on President Theodore Roosevelt's selection of Washington as a presidential advisor, Miller noted (in another essay titled "Roosevelt and the Negro") "where the patronage is, there the subservience of the politician will be also." The recourse to politics puts the black population in the hands of a small, elite group of leaders who may not be as wise and honorable as Washington was.

Today the choice of black leaders appears to be based more on decisions made by the media and the loudest voices in the black community as to whose personality is the most pungent and likely to make for stories with interesting conflicts with white conservatives. But the danger is just the same as it was in Miller's time: "This policy is not calculated to teach the Negro the needed lesson in self-government and manly political activity." On the contrary, Miller writes, "The Negro would remain in perpetual thralldom to an intermediary boss set up at the whim or caprice of whoever happens to be President," or, in the current case, whoever happens to own the *New York Times* and CNN.

Conservative blacks are trying to lead our people away from patronage, subservience, and victimization, into the American Dream of freedom, economic independence, and self-respect. The growth during these past few decades, although slow, has been real. The principles for which we argue would, if adopted, make for far more dramatic results. Black Americans must have the courage to break free from victimhood and the seeking of temporary favors, and instead make our way for ourselves, as Booker T. Washington argued so brilliantly. Only then will the promise of our civil rights truly be fulfilled.